SHELTERED BY GOD'S LOVE

52 BIBLE LESSONS FOR SENIOR ADULTS

MORTON KING

Abingdon Press
Nashville

SHELTERED BY GOD'S LOVE:
52 BIBLE LESSONS FOR SENIOR ADULTS

This book is printed on recycled, acid-free paper.

Library of Congress Cataloging-in-Publication Data

King, Morton Brandon, 1913–
    Sheltered by God's love : 52 Bible lessons for senior adults / Morton King.
        p.   cm.
    ISBN 0-687-04795-1 (alk. paper)
    1. Bible—Study and teaching.   2. Aged—Religious life.
I. Title.
BS600.2.K545   1997
220.6'1'0846—dc21   96-37714

Unless otherwise noted, Scripture quotations designated NRSV are taken from
the New Revised Standard Version Bible, Copyright 1989 by the Division of
Christian Education of the National Council of the Churches of Christ in the
USA. Used by permission.
    Those designated RSV are from the Revised Standard Version of the Bible,
copyright 1946, 1952, 1971 by the Division of Christian Education of the
National Council of the Churches of Christ in the USA. Used by permission.
    Those designated GNB are from the *Good News Bible*—Old Testament:
Copyright © American Bible Society 1976; New Testament: Copyright ©
American Society 1966, 1971, 1976. Used by permission.
    Those designated NEB are from *The New English Bible*. Copyright © The
Delegates of the Oxford University Press and The Syndics of the Cambridge
University Press 1961, 1970. Reprinted by permission.
    Those designated TAB are from the Amplified New Testament, © The
Lockman Foundation 1954, 1958, 1987. Used by permission.
    Those designated KJV are from the King James Version of the Bible.

99 00 01 02 03 04 05 —— 10 9 8 7 6 5 4 3 2

MANUFACTURED IN THE UNITED STATES OF AMERICA

To

my students at Wesleyan Nursing Home,
including

Mrs. Williams

Miss Hefner

Mrs. Gilmore

Mr. Byrd

Miss Parra

Mrs. Twidwill

ABOUT THE AUTHOR

Morton **King**, a retired professor of sociology from Southern Methodist University, has taught numerous collegiate and adult Bible-study classes. He developed these lessons with and for a group of residents at Wesleyan Nursing Home in Georgetown, Texas. In addition to a bachelor of arts in English literature and a master's degree in sociology from Vanderbilt University, he received his doctorate in sociology from the University of Wisconsin.

CONTENTS

Part I: The Old Testament

The God of Love and God's Relation to Us

The Psalms: Praise the LORD! He Loves Us

The Prophets: Words of Judgment and Forgiveness

Part II: The New Testament

The Long-Expected Jesus

Jesus: Light for the Whole World

Jesus Reveals a God of Steadfast Love

Lord, Teach Us to Pray

Divine Love Dies to Save Us

The Church of Jesus Christ

Part III: The Trinity

God in Three Persons

PREFACE

THESE BIBLE LESSONS HAVE A PURPOSE AND A HISTORY. The purpose is to present the Bible's proclamation and promise of God's steadfast and eternal love for all God's children. This message, the Good News of the Bible, is for anyone who wants or needs to know the Gospel. Here it is presented for mature adults, persons with much living behind them—some of whom are tired or lonely.

That purpose reflects the history. In 1989, a woman who was feeble in body but sharp and active mentally walked into Wesleyan Nursing Home in Georgetown, Texas. She was 99 years old.

After several weeks, she declared, "I taught Sunday school most of my life, the primary class. But I really don't know much about the Bible. Can you set up a class to teach us about the Bible?"

Challenged by the activities director, I answered that call: "Where can I find serious study material aimed at this population?" The director knew of none. (In the adult Sunday school literature we had been using there was an underlying theme: Get out into the world and do God's work!) Two year's search uncovered nothing to serve our purpose.

Therefore, I selected Scriptures for these 52 lessons during revitalized Bible study, guided by the Holy Spirit and aided by the Common Lectionary for the Christian Year. May your use of the lessons bring the same blessing to you that preparing them has for me.

Special thanks are due to many persons who helped and guided me. These include residents of Wesleyan Nursing Home who were my "fellow students."

The book is dedicated to a few of the most faithful. Essential support came from Mrs. Mamie Ruth Richter, Activities Director, and Mr. Chris Spence, President of Wesleyan Homes, Inc. They and their staff assisted both the development of the lessons and preparation of the book's manuscript. Lay and clerical friends read drafts and made useful corrections and suggestions.

A special debt is owed to three persons who many years ago introduced me, vividly and with power, to exciting messages in the Bible. One is a scholar, Bernard Anderson, whose study guide, *Unfolding Drama of the Bible,* has now gifted several generations. Two are preachers: William A. Smart and Clarence Jordan. They communicated the Bible's Good News to me in my native language, the English of Southern U.S.A.

INTRODUCTION

A CENTRAL MESSAGE OF THE BIBLE IS: "GOD IS LOVE." God loves us. God loves *you*. God takes care of us—yesterday, today, always. God's everlasting arms are stretched out to bear us up as on eagle wings. At the door of death, God stands, inviting us in. That is the Gospel, the Good News of the Bible.

The purpose of these lessons is to bring the Bible's message of love, forgiveness, and hope to persons in their mature years. Fifty-two lessons proclaim the "old, old story" of God's love. They are offered to guide serious group study in a variety of settings: Sunday school classes and small groups meeting in churches, private homes, retirement and nursing homes, or anywhere. *They also may be used by individuals for personal study and devotion.*

Each lesson begins and ends with a prayer. Each contains suggestions in **bold type** at points where Scripture passages may be read, using the Bible translation(s) of one's choice. The meaning may be clarified by reading more than one translation. Scripture quotations are from the New Revised Standard Version unless otherwise noted. Following the closing prayer are life-application questions.

Throughout, LORD appears in capital and small capital letters when it stands for God's Holy Name (see Lesson 2). For centuries, devout Jews have believed that God's Holy Name is too sacred to be spoken out loud. Even when reading Scripture in synagogue or temple, they substitute the words "the LORD" rather than saying the Name. Most English translations of the Old Testament show the same awe and reverence. I have chosen to use this style as well, to honor the Godhead, the One Unified and Ultimate Being who loves us enough to share his personal name with us. (When referring to God or specifically to Jesus as Lord, the capitalized lowercase is used.)

These Bible lessons were written to communicate God's unconditional love for all His children. May the Holy Spirit help you to know that these gifts are for you!

11

A WORD TO TEACHERS

SEVERAL YEARS AGO, I AGREED TO LEAD A GROUP OF mature adults in serious Bible study. I wanted material aimed at the special needs of this age group, material that emphasizes the Bible's Word of love, forgiveness, and hope. Unable to find it, I searched Scripture for passages that communicated "God loves you; loves everyone, everywhere; today, tomorrow, always." Through revitalized Bible study, with guidance from the Holy Spirit, I developed the lessons in this book.

The theme of God's steadfast forgiving love is repeated throughout all the lessons. That is only part of the whole Word, but the part my group wanted, and needed, to hear. Those who know "the old, old story" of God's love hunger to hear it again and again.

Several considerations guided my choice of content and vocabulary. Traditional God language has been used; most mature adults are comfortable with it. Likewise, the theology and doctrines are very orthodox, some might say "old-fashioned," so as not to disturb the foundation of anyone's faith, but build upon it. Even so, I have attempted to open up the Scriptures for new and deeper meaning—especially such familiar passages as Psalm 23 and the Lord's Prayer. I also have attempted to be as ecumenical as possible.

Against that background, here are some suggestions that may be of assistance to you:

~Remember, you are the leader of a particular group. What you have in these pages is "me," the way I think and talk. You are you and must be flexible and creative to serve your students effectively in your setting. That is, be adaptable, informative, interesting, and caring. The Spirit is there to guide, support, and inspire you—often through one or more of your students.

~The lessons are intended to be brief. From start to finish, each lesson averages about twenty-five minutes. They can be shortened or expanded as appropriate for different groups or different situations. You may find that a review of key ideas or themes from previous lessons would be helpful to your group.

~Allow time before and after the lesson for friendly "visiting." One benefit of participating in a group is the opportunity for Christian fellowship. You can be an instrument of God's love by showing genuine care and support. Show appreciation to individual members for their attendance and participation. In some groups, it may be appropriate during greetings and good-byes, to show such signs of friendship and support as a handshake, pat on the shoulder, or a hug.

~Begin and end each lesson with prayer. You may use these or create your own, in advance or spontaneously at lesson time. The opening prayers provided are varied. Some serve as preparation for the lesson; some reflect the season (either of nature or of the Christian Year); others resulted from some personal prompting. All the closing prayers attempt to lift up the kernel of that lesson. Paul wrote (Romans 8:26*b*) "We do not know how to pray as we ought." But we have to try, with help from the Holy Spirit.

~Some of your students may have vision, hearing, or other limitations. Reading even large print may be difficult for some. Remember to read the Scripture passages slowly, distinctly, and loudly enough for all to hear. Encourage students to bring their Bibles and follow along. If appropriate, suggest that they read the lesson's passages in advance.

~I have found that the most effective way to present the Scripture is to read it *during* the lesson, after introductory comments. Sometimes I read one short passage, comment, then move on to others. Lessons 35 and 50 are examples of that procedure. Use your judgment about whether to read all or some of the suggested Scripture in a lesson, or to add others you think germane. Experiment to find the best approach for your group.

~You will choose the Bible translation or translations you and your group prefer. I have found it rewarding to read a passage in several translations, until God's Word becomes clear to me. You may decide that a particular Scripture is communicated best by one particular translation. A number of scholarly English translations or versions are readily available. Most often, I depend on the *Good News Bible: Today's English Version* (GNB) and the *New Revised Standard Version* (NRSV). (The NRSV is quoted in the lessons, unless otherwise noted.) The Word sometimes sounds most clearly in the *Revised Standard Version* (RSV), in *The New English Bible* (NEB), or in the beloved *King James Version* (KJV). I work with all these and several others. You may wish to become acquainted with the Roman Catholic *New American Bible* (NAB) and *The Amplified Bible* (TAB).

~Consider the wishes of your group and your style of presentation to determine whether to have questions and discussion during or after the lesson. The questions with each lesson invite people to consider how the material connects with their own beliefs, habits, and life experiences. Encourage members to share thoughts, feelings, personal stories, and questions.

Like me, you will not know all the answers! Some answers may come from members themselves; others may require research by you or by one or more members. Your role is to encourage their desire and effort to learn and grow.

~If you and your group wish to follow the Christian Year, many of the New Testament lessons can be so used: for Advent, lessons 20–24; Epiphany, 25–27; Lent, 38–43; Pentecost, 44–48; Trinity, 49–52.

May the Holy Spirit inspire and guide you in communicating the Bible's Good News of God's forgiving love to hungry minds and hearts.

Part I
THE OLD TESTAMENT

THE GOD OF LOVE AND GOD'S RELATION TO US

1

God Revealed in Creation

Genesis 1:1-2, 3a; Psalm 8:1a, 3-5;
Psalm 19:1-4

OPENING PRAYER: Eternal God, Creator of all that is: You give us earth and sky, day and night, summer heat and cooling breezes. You give us sunshine and rain. In our health and in our sickness, you surround us with your love. You are our Savior, our Guide, and the Rock to which we cling in times of trouble or despair. You created us in love, and you care for us with your love. We are thankful. Therefore, we pray together, using the words your Son Jesus taught us, saying The Lord's Prayer . . . .

LESSON: The Scriptures teach us many important things. One of the most important is what God is like—his nature and the nature of his relationship with us. Therefore, we begin our study of the Bible's Good News with a section of lessons that may help us understand God better. The general theme: Our God reveals himself to us so that we can have a personal relationship with him. He reveals himself in creation; to human individuals; through the Prophets; in Scripture; and especially in Jesus his Son, whom we call Christ and Lord.

First, we focus on God's revelation by and through his creation. We see the wisdom and power with which God created this remarkable universe in which we live. He is also revealed today when we experience the world of nature he created. So we begin with the first verses in Genesis.

The Hebrew writer of this exciting chapter gave the world one of the greatest prose poems in all literature. It is a sublime majestic account, a hymn of praise to the creating God and to his wisdom, power, and glory. It tells us that the God we worship is transcendent, high and lifted up; above all, over all. Listen to its rhythms and ideas. It is beautiful, inspiring, and humbling. (**Read Genesis 1:1-2, 3a.**) There is little one can add to that. It tells us that we have a wise God who acts with power. He has only to speak a Word, and things happen. We are awed by his majesty and glory.

Two familiar psalms, 8 and 19, tell in moving poetry how a human being, a child of God created in God's own image, reacts when the hand of God is seen in nature. It speaks to us of God, of his nature and relationship with us. (**Read Psalm 8:1a, 3-5.**)

The psalmist, experiencing the excellent majesty of God's created world, was humble, in awe. We should be, too. Who are we to boast? When we see ourselves as God sees us, we are embarrassed, sometimes ashamed. And yet, God *values* us. He has given us an important place in his total scheme of things. (**Read Psalm 19:1-4.**) The psalmist here tells us that we can see God in the world he created, then stand in awe before his power and majesty. We sing "Praise God from whom all blessings flow."

To summarize: These Scriptures show us that God is wise and powerful. He is above all, over all. We are his children, who inherit some part of his image, his nature. We feel humble and unworthy when we compare ourselves to him. Yet we are his, we belong to him. He is "mindful" of us, pays attention to us. He loves and cares for us—all the time, whoever we are and whatever we do. Praise the LORD!

CLOSING PRAYER: Eternal God: You made this glorious universe and gave it to us, children created in your image. It provides us with all we need: food, work, beauty, challenges, awareness of your majesty, and especially of your love. We are thankful, Father, and praise your Holy Name. Amen.

Questions for Reflection or Discussion

1. **(Read Genesis 1:26-27.)** How does it make you feel when the Bible tells you that you are created in the image of God? Important? Talented? Responsible? Thankful? Proud? Humble?
2. Both males and females were created in God's image. How does that affect the way you: Think of what God is like? Talk about God? Think about men? About women?
3. Remember your personal experiences in and with the world of nature created by God: trees and flowers; birds and animals; sun, moon, stars; the weather [soft breezes, rain, storms]; rivers; mountains; sunrise; everything. What has nature revealed to *you* about its Creator?

2
God Speaks to Moses from a Burning Bush

Exodus 2:23–3:15

OPENING PRAYER: Eternal, creating God: Open our minds and our hearts to your presence among us. You are right here, closer than our hands or feet. You are with us *all* the time—in the air we breathe, in the food we eat, and especially in the Scriptures we study. Open our hearts and minds, that we may hear your Word, the personal word you have for each of us today. Help us to hear it, so that we may know you better and have a closer relationship with you. We ask this in Jesus' name, who taught us to pray together, saying The Lord's Prayer . . .

LESSON: We continue our study of the nature of God and of his relationship with us. Lesson 1 showed he is a God who reveals himself. He does not hide in heaven. He makes known to us what he is like and what kind of relationship he wants with us. He is a creating God. By creating the universe, he revealed his wisdom, his power, and his glory. This lesson emphasizes that God reveals himself to *individuals*. God revealed himself to Moses in a very special way. He spoke out of a burning bush on the side of a desert mountain.

Moses had an unusual history. He was one of those descendants of Abraham called Hebrews, "children of Israel," now slaves in Egypt. Pharaoh feared a revolt, so he ordered that all the Hebrew boy babies be killed. Moses' mother hid him for three months, then floated him on the Nile River in a basket. Pharaoh's daughter came to take a bath and found him. She took Moses home to the palace and educated him as a noble Egyptian.

Thus he was a man caught between two worlds. When he was grown, he saw an Egyptian whipping a Hebrew slave. He killed the taskmaster and ran away into the desert of Midian. There he married and was a shepherd caring for his father-in-law's sheep.

(**Read Exodus 2:23–3:15.**) This gripping story tells us several very important things about God and the way he relates to us.

1. God *hears* his children when they cry out to him in distress, when they groan in any kind of trouble. That is true for individuals as well as for nations. God hears us when we are in distress and cry out to him.

2. God not only hears, he *cares.* He cares about all his children. He takes care of you and me. That is the best definition of love: concern for another person; caring and helping. However, because he loves us, he does not give us all we want, but what in his wisdom he knows is best for us in the long run.

3. When God helps a group of people, he often picks one person to be a leader, a spokesperson for him. That person may seem to have few skills for the job. Moses could not speak effectively. Amos was a poor rancher, out on the edge of the desert. Jonah ran in the opposite direction, until he was swallowed by a big fish. Jeremiah was a teenager. Usually, God calls those with special skills. Moses, for example, knew both Hebrews and Egyptians.

In any case, God picks a person and says, "Now go and do it!" Usually, like Moses, the person asks "Why me, Lord? Not me!" But God promises to go with them, to guide, help, and empower them.

4. Most important, God revealed his personal, Holy Name to Moses. He revealed himself as a person, a person with whom we too can have a personal relationship. He is a God who draws close to human beings. He risks letting us get close to him. Our behavior often causes him pain, but that is all right with him; he wants to have a close, "first-name" relationship with us.

5. There are two very important things we need to know about God's Holy Name. First, it is a Hebrew word, formerly prounounced "Jehovah." Now scholars say it should be "Yahweh," which sounds like the Hebrew verb "I am." You remember that he said, "I AM WHO I AM" (Exodus 3:14). Hebrew words have rich, complex meanings. It also can mean "I will be who I will be." That is, God is ageless, eternal, from the beginning, now, and on past the end of time.

Martin Buber, a Jewish scholar, traced the Hebrew verb that means "I am" back through all the ancient writings he could find. He became convinced that in revealing this name, God told us not only that "I am," "I exist," but also that "I am *present*," and "I *shall be* present." God was, and is, present in his creation; he is present with us; he will be present with all his children forever.

Second, God's personal name is sacred, holy. It must not be used "in vain." For centuries, devout Jews have believed that the Name is too sacred to be spoken out loud. Even when reading Scripture in synagogue or temple, instead of saying the name out loud, they substitute the words "the LORD." Most English translations of the Bible show the same awe and reverence by using "LORD" in the Old Testament. Psalm 23 begins: "The LORD is my shepherd"; that is, it begins with God's holy personal name. The first verse of Psalm 8 reads, "O LORD [the name] our Lord [the one who rules our lives], how excellent is thy name in all the earth!" (KJV).

To summarize God's message from the burning bush: God gave us his personal name, made himself available to be with us. God loves us. He cares, especially for those who cry out to him in any kind of distress. He will help us.

CLOSING PRAYER: O LORD, our Lord: We are thankful that we can have a personal relationship with you. You love us, you hear us when we cry out to you, you take care of us—now and forever. Thank you, LORD; we praise your Holy Name. Amen.

Questions for Reflection or Discussion

1. What difference does it make to you that God's holy personal Name means "I am"? Does the "I shall be present" translation mean more to you, giving you more hope each day?
2. How does it affect your understanding of Scripture to know that, in the Bible, the "LORD" stands for God's personal Name?
3. How does it make you feel to know that God listens to us and hears our "groans," our cries for help?
4. Have you, personally, experienced God's presence—his care, his love? In what ways?

3
God Speaks to All Kinds of People

Genesis 3:6-9; 1 Samuel 3:3-10; 2 Kings 2:1-12a;
Jeremiah 1:4-9; Matthew 19:14; Luke 1:28-38, 2:22-38

OPENING PRAYER: Father: We are gathered again in your presence, seeking your Word in Scripture. We are thankful that you love us and care for us. We pray that your Holy Spirit will now open our minds and hearts, and lead us to hear and accept the message you have for us today. Help us to understand that you are concerned for everyone, for all kinds of people: old and young, women and men, rich and poor, good and bad. All of us are your children. You want to be in close touch with each one of us, and we are thankful. Therefore, we pray as Jesus taught us, saying together The Lord's Prayer . . . .

LESSON: What is God like? God is so big, so holy, so wise, so powerful, so loving that we cannot know and understand him completely. However, God has made known enough about himself for us to be in personal relationship with him. He makes himself available to us.

The Bible tells of all kinds of people to whom God has spoken. Often he has called them by name. They have been old folks and children; women and man; the poor and the rich; the righteous, and yes, even the sinful. It has been so since the very beginning, in the Garden of Eden.

Eve ate the forbidden fruit and shared it with Adam. They had sinned; they were innocent no longer: "The eyes of both were opened" (Genesis 3:7). They knew that they were naked, and they felt unfit to be in God's presence—even when covered with fig leaves. So they ran and hid among the trees. And what did God do? He came looking for them, calling, "[Adam!] Where are you?" (3:9). The very first people God called were sinners.

God speaks to all ages. Jesus said, "Let the little children come to me" (Matthew 19:14). Samuel was a little boy, apprenticed to Eli, an old blind priest. **(Read 1 Samuel 3:3-10.)** God called the boy Samuel to be his prophet, a relationship which lasted until Samuel was an old man. The prophet Jeremiah was a teenager when God called him. **(Read Jeremiah 1:4-9.)** God speaks differently to different individuals. To Jeremiah he gave firm commands. His angel messenger spoke gently to Mary, the mother of Jesus. **(Read Luke 1:28-38.)** When he speaks, God may command or simply make a request. He may only state the facts. He may speak firmly or gently.

God may have a special place in his heart for older people; he usually speaks gently to them. He arranged for two older people to be among the first to recognize the baby Jesus as the long-expected Messiah, when Joseph and Mary presented him at the Temple in Jerusalem. One was a woman, Anna, a widow for many years, 84 years old. The other was Simeon. **(Read Luke 2:25–32.)**

"Let your servant go in peace" (Luke 2:29 GNB). That is the way all of us would like to depart for the heavenly Kingdom to be with God. We would like for it to be a peaceful journey. There are other ways, however, and we have little choice but to trust the loving wisdom of God. When the prophet Elijah was old, God called him across the river Jordan into a desert place. **(Read 2 Kings 2:1, 7–11.)** There are many roads to heaven. Some are peaceful. Some may be rocky. A few may be as exciting as Elijah's ascent. In every case, however, God is calling one of his children home to be close to him.

From birth to death, and beyond, God is reaching out to each of us. He created us; we are his children. He loves us all, and he seeks us out to have a personal relationship with him—every one of us. Thanks be to God!

CLOSING PRAYER: O God, our loving Father: We are thankful that you know each of us by name and love us all. You call us into close relationship with you. We pray that, as the old hymn says, we may be "Close to Thee":

Lead me through the vale of shadows,
 bear me o'er life's fitful sea;
then the gate of life eternal `
 may I enter, Lord, with thee. Amen.

Questions for Reflection or Discussion

1. How does it make you feel to know that God speaks to all kinds of people? What kind of person are you?
2. How does God's "tone of voice" differ when he speaks to different persons under different circumstances? If he has spoken to you, how did he speak, and what did he say? If God should speak to you in the future, what might he say? What "tone of voice" might he use?
3. Simeon, after he had seen Jesus, was ready to depart, to die; but he wanted to "go in peace." Was Elijah's departure peaceful? How would you prefer your trip to heaven to be?
4. What are the ways a person can become closer to God? Do you practice any of these? Could you?

4
The Wideness of God's Mercy

Jonah 1:1-17; 2:1-10; 3:1-5, 10; 4:1-11

OPENING PRAYER: Eternal Creating God: You created everything that exists: the land and all its animals that live on the land. You created rivers, seas, and everything that swims. You created the sky and all the birds that fly in the air. You created us, male and female, in your own image. We feel your presence in your whole creation. Anywhere we go, you are there: on the highest mountain or down in the depths of the sea. You are there with us, day and night. You love and care for each one of us, and we are thankful. Therefore, we pray together as Jesus taught us, saying The Lord's Prayer . . . .

LESSON: We find an important message about God in one of the shortest and least understood books in the Bible, Jonah. We all "know" the whale swallowed Jonah; that he lived three days in its belly; and then was spit out on dry land, alive. It is important for us to know the whole story, to hear the deep Word of God that this Scripture communicates to us. The few verses selected for reading summarize the fast-paced action of the story.

(**Read Jonah 1:1-3.**) To understand this passage, we need answers to two questions:

1. Why didn't the prophet Jonah want to go to Nineveh?
2. Why did he think he could run away from God?

Early peoples thought that their own god's control was limited to a special territory. The children of Israel met their God at Mt. Sinai. He went with them to Canaan. His presence with them was symbolized by the Ark of the Covenant, installed in Solomon's temple at Jerusalem. He was their God; this was their land and his territory.

The Philistines, Babylonians, and others each had their territory and their god or gods. Nineveh was the capital of Assyria, an enemy country, east across the desert.

So Jonah thought, "What does *my* God have to do with those *foreigners*? I don't want to help my enemies. I'll get out of this Hebrew god's territory." Spain, at the west end of the Mediterranean, looked like a good place to hide. So Jonah *thought* he had bought a ticket to safety.

(**Read Jonah 1:4-5, 7, 11-12, 15-17; 2:1, 10.**) The book's main message begins here, forcefully and dramatically. God's territory, his concern and his control, did not end at the shoreline. He was also out there on the sea, in control of winds and waves—and a big fish. (Not a word here about any whale!) Jonah learned that God was at the bottom of the ocean, in the belly of a fish. He recognized God's presence and prayed. God was in control, and the fish spit Jonah out. He got a second chance.

(**Read Jonah 3:1-4.**) Jonah must have been glad to announce the destruction of these enemies of his people. But there was a certain reluctance. Why didn't he walk all through the city, preaching as he went? Was he afraid they might repent? What if God forgave them?

(**Read Jonah 3:5.**) Even the Ninevites heard God's voice. They not only heard; they *believed* God's message. They repented, *all* of them, from the king on down. They, too, were God's children.

(**Read Jonah 3:10.**) God forgave them. He forgives all his children. And how did Jonah like this? He didn't!

(**Read Jonah 4:1-5.**) In verse 2, Jonah quotes from Exodus 34:6. Jonah had read there that God is loving, merciful, forgiving. But apparently he believed that this applied only to Jonah's own people. He did not want those he hated to be God's children, too. Angry with God, he prays to die. God answers that prayer with a pointed question: "Is it right for *you* to be angry?" Jonah, instead of answering, goes out into the country, builds a booth, sits down, and sulks. How did God react to that? Remember that Assyria was, and is, a hot, dry, windy country.

(**Read Jonah 4:6-11.**) Right there, the book of Jonah ends abruptly. God tried to teach Jonah, not with words, but with a vivid example: a helpful plant which flourished briefly, then withered and died. Jonah felt sorry for the plant. He had not created, or even cultivated it; but he wanted it to live and grow and do its good work. How much more, God said, do I feel sorry for these people that I created. They have been wicked, but they are mine. I love them and forgive them, too.

Did Jonah learn this lesson? The Bible doesn't say. However, this little book contains important messages about God and the way he relates to us. God has power over the whole world. All people are God's children. He calls each person into some special relationship with him. God loves all his children. His love, his care, and his forgiveness cover all of us, even you and me. That's the Gospel Truth, the Good News of the Bible.

CLOSING PRAYER: O God, Father of our Lord Jesus Christ: We are thankful that you are the Lord of all creation and that we are your children. We are thankful that you are a loving, merciful God, always patient, always kind, always ready to forgive instead of punish. We are thankful that you are Father of all human beings, *our* loving Father, that you love and care for each of us. Amen.

Questions for Reflection or Discussion

1. Did Jonah teach you anything new? About God? What is the most important thing you learned?
2. Jonah tried to run away from God and God's power. Have you, or someone you know well, tried to do that? How? With what result?
3. Do you really believe that *your* God is ready to change his mind and relent from punishing? Under what circumstances does he do that?
4. Do we accept God's love for the people we consider our enemies? Or are we a lot like Jonah?
5. What message does Jonah have for us about God's love for people who are different; ones we dislike or fear? What are the implications for the Church? For our personal behavior?

5
God Revealed by the Psalmist

Psalm 145

OPENING PRAYER: Dear Heavenly Father: We are thankful that where even two or three are gathered in your name, you are there. You are present with us here. Help us to be aware of your Presence; aware of your steadfast love which blesses us; aware of your Holy Spirit, which inspires us and helps us hear your Word in Scripture. Open our minds and hearts so that we can learn what you want us to know about you. Because you love us, because you watch over us and take care of us, we praise your Holy Name. Now hear us as we pray together the words Jesus taught us, saying The Lord's Prayer . . . .

LESSON: We have been searching the Old Testament to learn more about the nature of God and the kind of relationship he offers us. Psalm 145 tells us several important things about God. It is a hymn of praise, reminding us that God is worthy of our praise. It was used in the worship of the Jewish Temple in Jerusalem. Parts of it were chanted by the priest, and other parts by the congregation. The passages spoken or chanted by the priest tend to be longer; there the priest refers to himself as "I" and to God as "You." (Even though he says "I," he is actually speaking for all the worshipers.)

Most of the congregation's passages are shorter and refer to God in the third person. The words of the people themselves are a kind of creed, a statement of what they believe God is like. They recognize and affirm God's nature: his greatness; his constant love and compassion; his goodness, especially to people in trouble; his caring attention to the cries of those in need. These are among the great affirmations of faith in the Bible. Scholars believe that verses 3, 8-9, 13*b*-14, and 17-20 were spoken by the people; the rest were spoken by a priest.

(Read Psalm 145.) [Note: If you are studying in a group, the teacher or one member might read the priest's part, while everyone else reads the people's part in unison. It might be helpful to read the psalm twice: once from the *King James Version,* and then from a modern translation such as *Today's English Version,* also known as the *Good News Bible.*]

The message of the psalmist, about God and his relationship to us, can be summarized this way:

1. The LORD is great and greatly to be praised; his greatness is beyond our understanding.

2. God forgives. The LORD is merciful, slow to anger. He is good to all.

3. God helps those who are in trouble; he lifts those who have fallen.

4. God listens. He is near to those who call to him; he hears their cries and saves them.

CLOSING PRAYER: We praise your holy name, O LORD. We are thankful that you are merciful and forgiving; that in your love you hear our cries and come to be near us, to help us. Praise the LORD! Amen.

Questions for Reflection or Discussion

1. What sights, sounds, experiences, or people have made you think "Praise the LORD!"? Have you ever said those words out loud? When? Describe the occasion.

2. Can you remember the occasion when you or someone you know well learned for the first time that God is "merciful, slow to anger"? That God is "good to *all*"? Describe the resulting reactions.

3. Describe some event in your own or someone else's life which convinced you that God lifts up those who have fallen. What were your reactions?

4. Describe a time when you called out to God and felt that he was near. How were you helped by God?

6
Created for Love

The Book of Ruth

OPENING PRAYER: We are thankful, Father, for this new day, and for the opportunity it gives us to come together and learn more about you as revealed in Scripture. You created us in your own image; we are your children. We are especially thankful that you are a loving Father who takes care of us. In Sunday school, we loved to sing "God will take care of you, along the way, through every day." We thank you, LORD, for the saving love you gave us in the life and the death of your Son, Jesus Christ, our Lord who taught us to pray together, saying The Lord's Prayer . . . .

LESSON: "God is love" is the central message of all the lessons. These three words capture the main theme of the whole Bible. We close this section on the nature of God and his relationship with us by looking at one of his children, a woman named Ruth. Ruth, who was created in God's image, showed her capacity for loving in her relationship with her mother-in-law. The message of this lesson is that *all* human beings—including you and me—are created by God and loved by God. We are capable of a loving relationship, both with God and with our fellow human beings.

Remember Ruth's story. There was a Hebrew man, of the tribe of Benjamin, who had a wife and two sons. They lived near Bethlehem. During a very bad drought, in danger of starving, he decided to move to a foreign country, Moab, east across the Jordan River. The people there spoke a different language and worshiped different gods. Elimelech and his wife Naomi lived there for several years, during which time their sons grew up and married Moabite girls.

Elimelech died, as did his sons—before they had children. Widowed and in a foreign land, Naomi was alone, without male kinfolk or support of any kind. So she decided to go back home, where she and her husband had relatives. When she told her two daughters-in-law her plans, she urged them to stay in their own country with their own families. She advised them to remarry men who spoke their language and practiced their religion. At that time, there was no place for a woman except in the home of a man, whether it be husband, father, or brother.

(Read Ruth 1:6-9, 14, 15.) This was a sad moment; all three women cried. One daughter-in-law decided to stay. The other, Ruth, said, "No, I will go with you." Naomi begged her to stay; one translation says "entreated" her. However, Ruth felt love as well as duty toward this lonely older woman who had no one to support her, and she spoke these beautiful words. **(Read Ruth 1:16-19a.)**

What made this depth of love possible? First, Ruth was created in the image of God, with a capacity for loving. Second, Naomi obviously had been a loving mother-in-law, and that love elicited Ruth's own loving response. These two things made it possible for Ruth to leave her native country, family, friends, and any prospects for a future husband to go into a foreign country, where she would worship a new God and face an unknown and uncertain future. Such love is its own reward. Often there is no other reward.

In Ruth's case, there is a happy ending. Back in Judea, Naomi set out to find Ruth a husband and a secure home. She arranged for Ruth to meet Boaz, a distant relative and a prosperous land owner. They married. Their son Obed was the grandfather of King David, from whose family line and lineage Jesus was born in Bethelehem.

Like Naomi and Ruth, we, too, are capable of reflecting the love of God on the people around us. We do not need to earn God's love; yet when we have experienced the saving love of God in Jesus, we are freed and empowered by the Holy Spirit to love others as God first loved us.

CLOSING PRAYER: Gracious God, our loving Father: We thank you for the beauty and mysteries of love. We are grateful for our capacity for loving, which you gave us when you created us in your own image. Help us to love all our neighbors, following the example of Jesus Christ, your Son, our Lord and Savior, in whose name we pray. Amen.

Questions for Reflection or Discussion

1. The Bible's meaning of "love," best demonstrated by Jesus, is caring concern for another person, often to the point of self-sacrifice. Ruth had this kind of love for Naomi. What is the best example of this kind of love you have observed in someone you know?
2. One's natural capacity for loving is often stimulated, released, empowered by receiving love from someone else. Have you ever seen that happen? Have you experienced it in your own life? Please describe the events.
3. Can you remember and describe a time when self-sacrificing love was its own reward, and no other was received? A time when such sacrifice was rewarded? How?
4. Do you see any significance in the fact that Ruth, a Moabite, an outsider, was an ancestor of Jesus? What?
5. Do you have any unusual ancestors in your family? How has God worked through them?

7

The LORD Is My Shepherd and Gracious Host

Psalm 23

OPENING PRAYER: We are thankful, Heavenly Father, for Scripture, whose words bring us your Word. They are words that reveal your divine nature and what our relationship with you is meant to be. We thank you for those who wrote these words which mean so much to us. We are especially thankful for the poets who wrote the hymns we call psalms. They tell us that you love us; that you provide what we need; that you protect us and guide us through life. Be with us today as we search for your Word in Scripture. And now we pray, together, using the words Jesus taught us, saying The Lord's Prayer . . . .

LESSON: With Psalm 23, we begin a series of lessons on the psalms. They are poems, hymns intended to be sung in worship. The book of Psalms actually is a collection of five books, 150 poems in all. The 23rd Psalm is perhaps the best known and best loved poem in the world. It has a special importance as a statement of faith in the God who loves us and takes care of us.

How do we talk about what God is like? We cannot see him. His majesty, power, glory, and love are too immense for us to capture in mere words. Yet, God has revealed enough about himself for us to love and trust him. How, then, can we think and talk meaningfully about God and his relationship with us? As does Psalm 23, we use words out of our human experience as

32

symbols that suggest the divine realities of God's nature. We use ideas to point to things we cannot see or fully understand.

Psalm 23 uses two main symbols to illustrate God's relationship with us. The first is a shepherd. The psalmist pictures us as the sheep of God's pasture. God provides our basic needs; protects us with his rod and staff; guides us along the right paths through life, even though some are dark and dangerous. The second symbol is a Host. Here we are guests in God's home. He invites us to dinner in the mansion of his love, which has many rooms.

(Read Psalm 23.) [Note: If you are studying in a group, read the psalm together in unison.] Now let us look at the psalm verse by verse [author's paraphrase], stating in everyday words the meaning we find in this familiar, beloved Scripture.

The LORD *is my shepherd* (v. 1*a*). The psalm's first word is God's holy personal name. Psalm 23 quite properly begins by centering our attention on God in a personal way.

Because my shepherd is this God, *I have everything I need* (v. 1*b*). The key word here is "need." In his wisdom, God gives us not what we want, but what he knows we need. The psalm assures us that all our real needs will be met.

He takes me to feed in green pastures; he leads me to drink from quiet pools of pure water (v. 2). That is, God provides our basic needs, from the very best sources available. Of course, we do not eat grass or drink directly from a river. Those are symbols. They stand for all our basic human needs. We are taken where the best food is available. The familiar "still waters" used in several translations represents a Hebrew word which means that the water is not rushing by too fast to drink and is "pure," not muddy or salty.

So God provides for our basic needs; and as a result, *He revives my whole life, body and soul* (v. 3*a*). The Hebrew word usually translated "soul" in verse 3 means "life"—mental, physical, and spiritual. The psalmist assures us that God revives us totally when we are hungry and thirsty, whether mentally, physically, spiritually, or all three.

He guides me along the right paths as he promised (v. 3*b*). God's paths are the best ones to take us from where we are to where we ought to be. This applies to *all* life's decisions. Choosing a career or a spouse, deciding who to vote for, or how to invest one's extra money—every decision should follow a path on which God leads us. Several translations read that God leads us "for his name's sake." Does this mean that God leads us to promote his name? No! It means that God is true to himself. He is forever faithful to the Covenant in which he promised to be our God, who will lead, love, and take care of us. He does what he says. We can trust him.

Yes, even if I walk through the dark valley of pain and death, I will fear no evil (v. 4*a*). During bad times, I may be scared. But when I trust my Good Shepherd to guide me, I do not expect evil to result; I expect something good. As Paul wrote, "All things work together for good for those who love God, who are called according to his purpose" (Romans 8:28). Why is that so?

Because you are with me; your everlasting arms protect and comfort me (v. 4*b*). In biblical times, shepherds had two main tools. The rod was a heavy stick used to fight off animals and thieves. The staff had a crook to pull a sheep out of a ditch or thorn bush, or to guide a lamb along a path. The psalmist used these symbols to communicate God's loving concern for us. The most familiar symbols for God's "tools" are "hands" and "arms." To put the psalm into words with deep meaning for us, we can say, "I will fear no evil, your everlasting arms protect and comfort me."

This verse is a turning point in the psalm. Until now, the psalmist has talked *about* God, in the third person. Now, going through some dark shadowy valley, it becomes personal. The psalmist stops telling others about God and speaks to him directly, calling him by his holy personal name. After this verse, God is symbolized as a host. Beginning with verse 5, we are guests in the home of a gracious host, invited to a dinner table prepared before we arrive. We might say it like this:

You spread out life's good things before me like a public banquet (v. 5*a*). Even my enemies can see what God has prepared for me—a bountiful table covered with what I need, a table at which

God welcomes me as a valued guest. To communicate the significance of being God's guests, the psalmist used two unfamiliar symbols: olive oil poured on one's head and a cup poured so full of wine that it runs over. Olive oil, often perfumed, was expensive. It was used to dress the hair of a dusty traveler, to give a special, cordial welcome.

Anointment has been a powerful symbol through the ages. It represents selection for some special relationship and status. This psalm tells us that God considers us important and has selected us for some special relationship with him. We can "translate" it this way: *You mark me with your special favor* (v. 5*b*).

What about that too-full cup? Wine was a mainstay of the ancient diet. It was weak, with just enough alcohol to kill germs in the drinking water and provide calories. A host would continue to fill the wine cups (as we do iced-tea glasses and coffee cups) of guests he wanted to make especially welcome. Therefore we might say: *My life is like a cup filled to the brim and running over* (v. 5*c*). When we remember all that God has done for us since childhood, when we think of the way God still supports, protects, and comforts us, then our hearts overflow with gratitude.

Your goodness and kindness will surely follow me all the days of my life (v. 6*a*). God's love, mercy, and grace follow us, whether we walk in sunshine or in shadows. Wherever we go, God is with us; we are never alone. He is not "out there" somewhere, waiting for us to pray hard enough to get his attention. No! He *follows* us all the days of our lives.

And the psalmist says that his Presence does not end with death: "I will dwell in the house of the LORD forever" (v. 6*b* NIV). We call the church building, as the Jews did their Temple, "the house of the LORD." However, here the psalmist pictures God's love as a mansion, with enough rooms for everyone. That is our *future* home; but God, our Divine Host, also invites us to live with him *now*. His forgiving, steadfast love is a warm, protecting, comfortable home, with a room prepared and reserved for you and me. Therefore, the psalm's last beautiful line might be read, *And I will be at home in the house of God's love, forever*.

We could use the following words to express the meaning of the Twenty-third Psalm for us today:

The LORD is my shepherd;
I have everything I need.

He takes me to feed in green pastures;
he leads me to drink from quiet pools
of pure water.
He revives my whole life,
body and soul.

He guides me in the right paths
as he promised.
Yes, even if I walk through the dark valley
of pain and death,
I will fear no evil,
because you are with me;
Your everlasting arms protect and comfort me.

You spread out life's good things before me
like a public banquet.
You mark me with your special favor.
My life is like a cup,
filled to the brim and running over.

Your goodness and kindness will surely follow me
all the days of my life;
And I will be at home in the house of God's love,
forever.

CLOSING PRAYER: O God, our Heavenly Father: We acknowledge you as our Good Shepherd, as our provider, our protector, our guide. You are the divine host who invites us into your loving home to share your feast and your gracious hospitality, now and forever. We are thankful. Amen.

Questions for Reflection or Discussion

1. Have you experienced God in any of the ways the psalmist did? The Good Shepherd: Provider? Protector? Guide? The

Gracious Host: Showing special favor? Preparing the things you need? When? How?

2. "I shall not want"; "I have everything I need." Do you really feel that way? What is the difference between a want and a need? Why doesn't God give you everything you want and pray for?

3. The Bible says that you "will dwell in the house of the LORD forever." What does that mean to you now? What might it mean to you later? How does that make you feel?

4. If we are "at home in the house of God's love," how can we share this love with others? As individuals? As the Church?

8
Praise God
Who Creates and Teaches

Psalm 19

OPENING PRAYER: Eternal God our Father: You have given us so many things for which we are thankful. Your whole creation fills us with wonder at your wisdom, your power, your glory. There is the sun, the moon, and all the stars. There is sunshine and rain. There are trees and flowers, plants and animals. We are thankful for everything you created. We are especially thankful that you created us in your own image, to live and die as parts of your creation, sustained by your steadfast love. We are thankful, also, for the memories we have and for the hope you give us for the future, both in this life and the life to come. We are most thankful, O God, for your Son and our Savior, Jesus Christ, who died that we might have abundant eternal life with you. Therefore, we pray together, using the words he taught us, saying The Lord's Prayer . . . .

LESSON: We continue our study of the psalms with Psalm 19. This well-known psalm tells us important things about God and his relationship with us. It has three parts, each of which offers a different but valuable message:

1. The glory of God is shouted by the heavens he created.
2. God's teaching and commandments have value for our lives.
3. Realizing his failures, the psalmist offers a prayer of confession and requests God's help.

(Read Psalm 19:1-4, 7-10, 12-14.) [Note: It is suggested that you read these selected verses from the familiar King James Version. As we continue the lesson, the main points use modern language. As you read, remember that the psalm is poetry, a hymn to be sung or chanted in worship.]

"The heavens are telling the glory of God; and the firmament proclaims his handiwork" (v. 1). What is the "firmament"? The ancients believed in a small, tidy world: the earth was mainly flat and floated on deep water, stretching off in all directions. It was covered by a dome (firmament) which held up the waters above the earth. The sun, moon, and stars moved in or on the firmament.

Our picture of the universe is much larger and more complicated. Our round planet is one of several which circle a small sun, one star among billions which stretch away trillions of miles in every direction. The poet who wrote this hymn saw and heard the glory of God proclaimed by God's creation, as he understood it. Our understanding of this immense universe shouts, "Glory to God in the highest" much more loudly—if we listen.

The psalmist described the cosmic proclamation in this way: "Each day announces it to the following day; each night repeats it to the next. No speech or words are used, no sound is heard; yet their message goes out to all the world and is heard to the ends of the earth" (vv. 2-4 GNB). These poetic words tell us how the mystery of God is communicated to us by the silent voices of God's Creation.

The second part of the psalm speaks of the teachings, the instructions, of God, and how obeying them improves our lives. "The law of the LORD is perfect; it gives new strength. The commands of the LORD are trustworthy, giving wisdom to those who lack it. The laws of the LORD are right, and those who obey them are happy. The commands of the LORD are just and give understanding to the mind. Reverence for the LORD is good; it will continue forever" (vv. 7-9a GNB). God's holiness makes us stand in awe and reverence before him, and that is cleansing. Awareness of his power and love purifies us.

Third, the psalmist, after meditating on God's teachings and commands, says that "by them is your servant warned" (v. 11). We are thereby made aware of our weaknesses, failings, and sins—including some we had not noticed before; and that leads to prayer: "No one can see his own errors; deliver me, LORD, from hidden faults! Keep me safe, also, from willful sins; don't let them rule over me. Then I shall be perfect and free from the evil of sin" (vv. 12-13 GNB).

The psalmist shows us the glory and holiness of God revealed in creation. Then he reviews God's teachings and their value and importance to us. This leads him, and us, to be aware of our failings and to confess and be cleansed. Finally, when the psalmist becomes aware that he needs God's help to be the person he was created to be, he prays the short prayer so familiar to all of us: "Let the words of my mouth and the meditation of my heart be acceptable to you, O LORD, my rock and my redeemer" (v. 14).

CLOSING PRAYER: For our closing prayer today, let us repeat together those familiar words: "Let the words of my mouth and the meditation of my heart be acceptable to you, O LORD, my rock and my redeemer." Amen.

Questions for Reflection or Discussion

1. What message from God, or about God, have you heard from the silent voices of the sky, the clouds, the sun and moon and stars which he created? The universe as we know it is immense, not flat and "tidy" as the psalmist understood it. Is the message it speaks to you the same as that the psalmist heard? In what ways is its message different?

2. The psalmist wrote that the law, the teachings, of God "give new strength," "give understanding and wisdom," "rejoice the heart," or "make happy those who obey them." Which of these are true for you? Which are not?

3. Have you ever been cleansed by your awe, your reverence for God? How and why did it happen? How long did your cleansing last?

4. When you think about the vast universe God created, about his commandments and teachings, does it lead you to pray? If so, how do your prayers compare with those of the psalmist?

9

Wait for the LORD,
a God We Can Trust

Psalm 27

OPENING PRAYER: We are thankful, Father, that when two or three of us come together in your name, we find your Holy Spirit waiting for us, ready to help us see, hear, and understand your Word in Scripture. Be with us now, O LORD, and bless our time together. Open our minds and hearts to receive your Word, the special word you have for each one of us today; for we pray together, using the words Jesus taught us, saying The Lord's Prayer . . . .

LESSON: The psalms are an important source of inspiration and comfort. Psalm 27 is a song of faith. Like the words of the old hymn, it proclaims that "God will take care of you, through every day o'er all the way." God *does* take care of us. Therefore, we need to trust God, to "wait on the LORD" (v. 14 KJV), patiently watching to see what he is doing for us and what he wants us to do for others.

(Read Psalm 27:1, 3-5, 7-9, 11, 13-14.) [Note: It is suggested that you read Psalm 27 from the King James Version. The verses quoted in the lesson are from modern translations for comparison.] "The LORD is the stronghold of my life; of whom shall I be afraid?" (v. 1*b*). The light of God's love shines into all the dark spots of life. Why should we fear anyone or anything? Since God protects us, we never need to be afraid. "For he will hide me in his shelter in the day of trouble; he will conceal me under the cover of his tent; he will set me high on a rock" (v. 5).

Sometimes we may fear that God has left us, but God's love is always spread over us, like the protecting wings of a mother hen, the safe covering of a sturdy tent. Our final, real safety is our secure place on top of the Rock of Ages "that is higher than I." Even when we know this in our minds, our hearts and our spirits may still be low. Often we feel "down" and lost, as this psalmist did. That is when the psalmist tells us to call out to God, to seek God in prayer. "Hear, O LORD, when I cry aloud, be gracious to me and answer me! Thou hast said, 'Seek ye my face.' My heart says to thee, 'Thy face, LORD, do I seek'" (vv. 7-8 RSV).

"Seek my face." God wants us to have a close, personal relationship with him. Even when we feel lost or separated from God by our sin—even when we are angry at God—he still says, "Seek me!" And way down deep in our hearts, we long to be close to him. Our heart cries, "I *do* seek you, LORD!" Hear the cry of the psalmist: "Do not hide your face from me. Do not turn your servant away in anger, you who have been my help. Do not cast me off, do not forsake me, O God of my salvation!" (v. 9).

Even in the depths of despair, the psalmist knew that God saves us. Recognizing this, we can rise out of the depths of our despair. As the old hymn says, "with healing balm my soul he fills." When we feel the balm applied, what do we say to God then? "Teach me your way, O LORD, and lead me on a level path" (v. 11). That is, be my Good Shepherd. With God in charge, we sense his love, we feel his comforting presence. Then our faith and confidence return. Like the psalmist, we can say: "I believe that I shall see the goodness of the LORD in the land of the living" (v. 13). Trusting God, we can have faith and not despair. We can be strong. With courageous hearts, we can wait for the LORD.

In the poetic language of the Bible, "waiting" means "trusting." Knowing that God is in control, we leave everything in his hands. Whatever our situation, whatever our problems, the secret of abundant life is this: Trust in the LORD.

CLOSING PRAYER: Yes, LORD: You are our shepherd, a Good Shepherd, our provider, protector, and guide. You are our light and our salvation. We are thankful that we do not need to be afraid. We can trust you. Under the tent of your love, we are safe. On the high rock of your salvation, we are secure. Thank you, LORD! Amen.

Questions for Reflection or Discussion

1. Does this psalm remind you of some favorite hymns? Can you sing them, or read the words, now?
2. "Wait on the LORD; wait for the LORD." This is one of the main messages of the Bible. Do you find it hard to "Wait on the LORD"? Why? When you do "wait," why do you do it? While you are "waiting," what do you think, feel, and do?
3. The LORD is your "light and salvation"; he will set you "high on a rock." When you remember that, what fears and anxieties diminish or even disappear?
4. Do you ever hear God say to you in Scripture, during prayer, or in any other way, "Seek ye my face?" In what ways do you respond in thought, feeling, or action?
5. The psalmist cried out to God, "Do not hide your face from me!" Do you ever feel like that? When? How do you "cry out" to God? How does he answer you?

10
Songs of Ascent and Access

Psalms 121 and 24

OPENING PRAYER: Eternal God, our loving Heavenly Father: We praise you for your world, this marvelous universe of sun and moon and stars. We praise you for your rich and varied forms of life: trees and flowers, butterflies and birds, animals of every kind; and for *our* life, human life. We know sunshine and rain, winter and spring, youth and old age, sorrows and joys. In all of this, you are always present: in the beginning, now, and forever. You are at our side. Your steadfast love surrounds us; your everlasting arms support and guide us. We are thankful. We are especially thankful for your forgiving love revealed in Jesus Christ our Lord, who taught us to pray together, saying The Lord's Prayer . . . .

LESSON: We continue our study of the psalms, which were poems to be sung or chanted. They were used in Temple worship for different purposes on different occasions. Psalm 121 is a "song of ascent." These psalms (120–134) were used by pilgrims as they traveled to Jerusalem for sacred festivals.

Residents of Jerusalem could go to the Temple every day. Some did. But if you lived in distant villages, visiting the Temple was a special, occasional event. That was especially true if you lived up north in Galilee. Between there and Judea in the south was a country called Samaria. Samaritans were despised by Jews. Jews avoided Samaritans and their territory.

Therefore a Jew going from Nazareth to Jerusalem would go around to the east, down the Jordan Valley to Jericho. From Jericho, it was a hard climb up to Jerusalem and Mt. Zion, on which the Temple was built. As they climbed up the steep road, the pilgrims thought about God, what he is like, and what he

44

does for his children. The 121st Psalm was sung while toiling up hill toward the Temple. Hot, tired, yet excited about being close to their journey's end, they sang.

(Read Psalm 121.) This is a beautiful, deeply felt expression of faith. God is worthy of our gratitude and praise. He loves and takes care of us. His eyes are never closed to us and to our needs. Day and night, his love protects us as we come and go, or as we stay.

(Read Psalm 24.) This psalm had a special place in Temple worship. It was used on a very special occasion. Once a year, the priests, king, and people rededicated the Temple as the place where God was enthroned. God's abiding Presence was in its Holy of Holies. To welcome God back into his Temple, a procession formed, including local residents and pilgrims. At the head of the procession, priests carried a sacred object which symbolized the coming of the LORD God Almighty to reoccupy his throne. Scholars suggest that the psalm began as the procession stood at the massive closed doors of the Temple.

The psalm has three sections, each with its own singers and its own particular message. It probably went something like this:

1. Verses 1 and 2 were used by both people and priests to praise the God they recognized as the Sovereign Lord of all that exists.

2. Verses 3 to 6 were a rite of purification. They asked, first, what should one be and do in order to worship this holy God "in spirit and in truth"? Two priests at the head of the procession may have chanted these verses. Remember that the Temple was on Mt. Zion.

One priest asked: "Who shall ascend the hill of the LORD? And who shall stand in his holy place?" (v. 3).

The other priest answered, as the people promised in their hearts, "Those who have clean hands and pure hearts, who do not lift up their souls to what is false, and do not swear deceitfully" (v. 4). Then a priest chanted words of forgiveness and declared that the assembled worshipers were fit to enter the house and the presence of the LORD: "The LORD will bless them and save them; God will declare them innocent. Such are the people who come to God, who come into the presence of the God of Jacob" (vv. 5-6 GNB).

3. Then priests and people moved up to the outer doors of the Temple itself. These doors, or gates, were wide and high; but still not big enough for the Lord of all Creation to pass through them. Therefore the cry went up: "Fling wide the gates, open the ancient doors, and the great king will come in" (v. 7 GNB). A priest asked: "Who is this great king?" (v. 8*a* GNB). Another answered, "The LORD, strong and mighty, the LORD, victorious in battle" (v. 8*b* GNB). Then perhaps all the priests chanted: "Fling wide the gates, open the ancient doors, and the great king will come in" (v. 9 GNB).

At that moment, as trumpets blasted, those mighty, ancient doors swung wide; and the High Priest who stood inside asked for the last time, "Who is this great king?" (v. 10*a* GNB). And all the people shouted, loudly and joyously, "The triumphant LORD—he is the great king!" (v. 10 GNB). Then priests and people filed into the Temple, eagerly seeking the Holy Presence they came to worship.

The whole psalm was sung or chanted, with support from a variety of musical instruments. We do not know for sure what instruments were used. Certainly there were trumpets and harps and loud clashing cymbals. You can be sure that it lifted up the hearts of those worshipers.

Perhaps you can remember some moment of worship when you were so moved that your scalp tingled. Perhaps it was some quiet moment, when you felt yourself alone in God's overwhelming presence. Maybe it was on Palm Sunday; or during an anthem such as the "Hallelujah!" chorus; or during a sermon. This psalm involved worshipers in a celebration of God's greatness, a celebration of the joy and excitement of being in his Presence. Our worship, too, can be moving and exciting.

CLOSING PRAYER: O God, we lift up our eyes and our hearts to you. We are thankful for your steadfast love and tender care. We come to you through the deep valleys and up the steep hills of our lives. You, whose wisdom and power created the world, go with us on our journey. When we come to our journey's end, you will be there waiting for us. Tired and discouraged as we often are, help us to remember that, inside the ancient doors of your heavenly home, there is joy and celebration in your Presence. We know, LORD, that you will keep us safe in all our comings and goings, now and forever. Thank you, LORD! Amen.

Questions for Reflection or Discussion

1. Did you learn something new about Psalm 121? About Psalm 24? What?
2. Both these psalms convey the eagerness with which faithful people sought to enter God's presence and worship him. Remember and describe an occasion when you eagerly anticipated either a regular or special worship service, or an approaching moment of private prayer. How did you feel? Why?
3. Does that hard uphill climb in Psalm 121 remind you of anything in your own past or present life? When life is a struggle, do you "lift up your eyes" to God? Have you been aware of the presence of the One who never sleeps?
4. How should we prepare to enter God's presence, at church or in private prayer? Is God present with us in all times and places? If so, what do we need to do to become aware of his Presence?
5. Is it easier for you to think of God as the great King, the LORD triumphant, or as a friend or elder brother, like Jesus? Is God both of these—and more?

11
Praise the LORD Who Blesses Us

Psalm 103

OPENING PRAYER: Creating God, who made the world and all it contains: You love all that you have made. You are present with us now, taking care of us and supporting us in your everlasting arms. We are thankful for all your many gifts, especially for your forgiving love revealed in Jesus Christ our Lord. You forgive our iniquities; you do not deal with us according to our sins. You are merciful, gracious, slow to anger, and abounding in steadfast love. For all this, we praise you and bless your Holy Name. Now we pray together, using the words Jesus taught us, saying The Lord's Prayer . . . .

LESSON: We continue our study of the psalms with the 103rd. As you read the psalm, notice that it is a powerful hymn of praise to God. God is to be praised, not just by human beings, but by all creatures in his universe. The poem begins on a very personal note: God forgives *me*, heals *me*, takes care of *me*. Then it moves out to the whole nation of Israel, especially the weak and oppressed; and finally to all creatures, both in heaven and on earth. It ends on a note of pure praise. **(Read Psalm 103.)**

The psalm begins: "Bless the LORD" (v. 1*a*). What does that mean? It is God who pours out his blessings on me, and on you. Who am I, what can I do, to give God "blessings"? The Hebrew word "bless" can also mean "praise." I can praise God in gratitude, thankful for what he has done for me, so verse 1 can be rendered: "Praise the LORD, O my soul! All that is within me, praise his holy name!" I am to praise God not only with my lips, not only with my soul, but with *all* that is within me.

The psalm continues: "Do not forget how kind he is. He forgives all my sins and heals all my diseases. He keeps me from the grave and blesses me with love and mercy. He fills my life with good things" (vv. 2*b*-5*a* GNB). We may not be able to see that God is doing all these things for us. We have aches and pains; worries, troubles, and fears. And we are aware that death is approaching. So it is hard for us to see that life is filled with good things. There is one thing, however, of which we can be sure: "He forgives all my sins" (v. 3*a* GNB).

God *wants* good things for us. God's love is at work for us all the time. When I am open to God's presence in my life, then I can see the ways his love and mercy are blessing me. I can see *some* good things that he has given me, no matter how dark it seems. And we know that eventually, God will call us into abundant eternal life with him in heaven.

The psalmist also teaches that God is especially concerned about the weak, the oppressed, the forgotten—all those persons with special needs: "The LORD judges in favor of the oppressed and gives them their rights" (v. 6 GNB).

Now the psalm moves on to its main point about God: "The LORD is merciful and loving, slow to become angry and full of constant love. He does not keep on rebuking; he is not angry forever. He does not punish us as we deserve or repay us according to our sins and wrongs. As high as the sky is above the earth, so great is his love for those who honor him. As far as the east is from the west, so far does he remove our sins from us" (vv. 8-12 GNB). The people of Israel sinned and lacked total commitment to God. But he still loved them and forgave them, as he loves and forgives us. That message is clear throughout the Bible.

Psalm 103 continues with this tender passage: "He knows what we are made of; he remembers that we are dust. . . . Our life is like grass. We grow and flourish like a wild flower; then the wind blows on it, and it is gone . . . . But for those who honor the LORD, his love lasts forever" (vv. 14-17 GNB).

A God like this deserves the praise of every creature everywhere:
>Praise the LORD, you strong and mighty angels . . .
>Praise the LORD, all you heavenly powers . . .
>Praise the LORD, all his creatures . . .
>Praise the LORD, my soul! (vv. 20-22 GNB)

CLOSING PRAYER: For our closing prayer, we use one of the ancient songs of the Church. Let us pray: Glory be to God on high, and on earth peace, goodwill to men. We praise you, we worship you, we glorify you. We give thanks to you for your great glory, O LORD God, heavenly King. Amen.

Questions for Reflection or Discussion

1. Praising God is one of the main functions of Christian worship. What are your favorite ways to praise God in a worship service?
2. What kinds of thoughts, feelings, and actions are involved when one "praises God"? What do you think about, how do you feel, what do you do when you praise God?
3. The psalmist praised God because "he fills my life with good things." Do you sometimes find it hard to believe that? Why? When you are worried, troubled, or afraid, is it possible to believe that God is giving you "good things"? What can change your disbelief to trust?
4. What evidence have you had in your own life that God is "merciful, loving, full of constant love which lasts forever"?
5. What difference does it make to us that all the creatures of every kind which God created praise him? Do we respect other parts of God's creation more?

12
Praise the LORD, Creator and Sustainer

Psalm 104

OPENING PRAYER: We praise you, O God, for all your works. You made the world and all that is in it. Your whole creation feeds and sustains us. We can trust you because you take care of us. Help us to be aware of your presence here, now, with us. Help us to hear your Word in Scripture, to welcome it with glad and open hearts. We pray all this in the name of Jesus, who taught us to pray together, saying The Lord's Prayer . . . .

LESSON: Psalm 104 is a long hymn of praise, telling us of God's wise creating power, of the orderly world he made for us to live in, and how he feeds and sustains all he created. It makes clear that we, like everything else, live in complete dependence upon God. Selected verses deserve special attention.

(Read Psalm 104:1-4, 10-19, 24, 27-30, 33.) The psalm speaks of God as a powerful and wise creator. It describes him as the maker of an orderly world, in which we can be at home. God's world is full of *life:* plants and trees, animals of every kind, and the human beings he created in his own image. We are an interconnected part of the complex web of life that God created.

The psalmist also praises God as Sustainer. God's loving care provides the oxygen we breathe, the water we drink, the food we eat; God provides everything we need to sustain our life. We are his children; he loves us and will give us all we really need. Because we can trust God, we feel like singing his praise as long as we live: "Bless the LORD, O my soul" (Psalm 104:1*a*).

CLOSING PRAYER: We praise you; we bless you; we give thanks to you for your great glory, O LORD God, heavenly King. In Jesus' name, we pray that you will keep our hearts full of the joy of your loving, sustaining presence. Amen.

Questions for Reflection or Discussion

1. What difference does it make in your daily life that God created an orderly world, where oceans, mountains, and rivers have their place; where the sun, moon, and stars know when to rise and set; and where day always follows night, and night follows day? What difference should it make?

2. What difference does it make to you that the earth is full of life (grass, plants, trees; animals, birds, fish) all living together in one interrelated web of life? What difference should it make?

3. Here are some facts to think about: You and I must breathe oxygen to live. Our bodies inhale oxygen and exhale carbon dioxide. Green plants must have the carbon dioxide for their life processes. They use it and release the oxygen our lives require. Elizabeth Barrett Browning, remembering Moses and the burning bush, wrote, "Every bush is aflame with God, but few take off their shoes." What are the psalmist and this English poet telling us about the nature of God, and about the nature of our relationship with the universe he created?

4. This psalm speaks of singing praise to God as long as we live. What are some of your favorite hymns of praise? Sing or read a couple of them now.

13
Prayers of Despair and Praise

Psalms 130, 111, 150

Opening Prayer: Our Heavenly Father: We are thankful for Scripture, which reveals to us who you are and the plans you have for us. Today, we thank you especially for the psalms. Some of the psalms are cries of anguish, prayers that rise up to you out of the depths of our despair. Others sing joyful praises to you, prayers of thanksgiving for your power, your holy justice, and especially for your steadfast, forgiving love. LORD, send now your Holy Spirit to us. Open our hearts and minds to the wisdom in these ancient songs. We ask these things in the Spirit of Jesus, who taught us to pray together, saying The Lord's Prayer . . . .

Lesson: This lesson concludes our study of the psalms, songs from the hymnbook that Jesus knew. We will study three short psalms. Two are songs of praise; one, an urgent prayer for help.

(Read Psalm 130.) This is a prayer for help. Its Latin name is *De Profundis* ("out of the depths") because of its opening words. While it begins as a cry of despair, it ends on a note of hope and faith. How often we, too, cry out to God from the depths of our worry, fear, pain, guilt, or even anger. It is comforting to know that a personal God hears us, a God who has told us his name. Desperately we want him to hear us, and he does. This psalm tells us that God hears us when we cry out to him; that he loves and forgives us; that we can believe God does care. Because we know that, we can wait for him in hope and confidence, as night watchmen wait for the dawn.

(Read Psalm 111.) This is a hymn of praise. In it, the poet remembers all that God has done and responds in praise and thanksgiving. Notice that it gives seven reasons for us to thank and praise God: God has power and majesty; great are all his works; God's righteousness and justice are everlasting; God is kind, merciful, forgiving; God provides us with food and meets our other basic needs; God's teachings are true and dependable, to be performed faithfully; God sets his people free—from sin and from evil; God inspires awe and reverence, the beginning of wisdom. It is no wonder that "He is to be praised forever" (v. 10 GNB).

(Read Psalm 150.) This psalm closes the book with a joyful shout of praise, celebrating God's greatness. Here we learn that worship is a celebration of God's power, wisdom, and love. This celebration can be worshiping in silence; it can be the singing of hymns old and new, quietly or loudly; it can be accompanied by the sound of trumpets, clashing cymbals, or guitars. Worship celebrates what God has done in the past; what he now does for all people; and what his wisdom, his power, and his love will do to the future.

CLOSING PRAYER: Dear Father, our Creator, Sustainer, Redeemer: We cry out to you in our anguish and distress and know that you hear us. You give us your personal attention. You care about us. Therefore, we can wait patiently in hope and faith. Your steadfast love surrounds us, night and day. You give us what you know is best for us. Thank you. With everything that breathes, we praise your Holy Name. Praise the LORD! Amen.

Questions for Reflection or Discussion

1. What is your favorite psalm? Why? What does it tell you about God and about his relationship with you?
2. Out of what kinds of "depths" have you cried out to God? What happened? How did God answer you?
3. Are there things about God and your relationship with him which cause you to praise the LORD? If so, list them. What did the psalmist experience that you have not? Why?
4. What kind of public worship do you prefer: quiet, active; what kinds of musical instruments; informal, formal ritual; something else?

14

Call to Covenant

Exodus 19, 20, 24

OPENING PRAYER: Creating God: You made us in your own image, both males and females. We are your children; you are our Father. Like a parent, you love us, provide what we need, and protect us from evil. You help us when we are in trouble. You teach us the right way to go. In your love, when we do not walk in your way, you forgive us and restore us to life with you. We are thankful, especially for your forgiving love revealed in the life, death, and resurrection of your Son, Jesus Christ. And now we pray together, using the words he taught us, saying The Lord's Prayer . . . .

LESSON: This is the first of six lessons on Old Testament prophets in the eighth century B.C. They are interesting men, called by God for a very important, but also unpopular, even dangerous, mission. God made them his spokesmen to proclaim his Word to those he brought out of slavery in Egypt to a promised land. We also find messages here for us, for our time. God made a covenant with Israel at Mt. Sinai. There God offered to be Israel's God, *if* the people would worship only him and live according to the Ten Commandments and his other teachings. They agreed, but they often broke that agreement. The central task of the prophets was to interpret the covenant; to warn of dangers that came from breaking the covenant; and to proclaim the promise of God's forgiving love.

(Read Exodus 19:1-12; 16-20; 20:1-21; 24:3-8.) Israel had accepted God's covenant. However, living up to it proved difficult. Many of the Israelites, including kings and priests, fell away from God and his commandments. They killed, committed adultery, took the property of widows and orphans, and committed other sins. At times, only a few Israelites remained faithful. That is where the prophets came in. Their job was to speak out and call the people back to faithful obedience. They proclaimed the word of judgment, describing the troubles and evils that would befall the Israelites if they continued in their sinful ways. They also proclaimed the word of promise, of hope, of love; the loving forgiveness God would give *if* the people returned to the covenant life. Their message made plain that to receive forgiveness means more than feeling guilty and saying, "I'm sorry!" It requires change of direction, a return to God's way.

The people did not like the prophets' message. They treated them badly, even killed them. Centuries later, Jesus told his disciples to expect trouble, "for so persecuted they the prophets which were before you" (Matthew 5:12*b* KJV).

Christians speak of the Mt. Sinai agreement between God and Israel as the Old Covenant. Jesus came to establish a New Covenant between God and all who say "yes" to God's offer: "If you will worship me alone and live obediently according to my teachings, I will be your God and you will be my people. I will love you, forgive you, take care of you." Each person can say "yes" or "no." The task of the Church, like that of the prophets, is to "speak forth," to proclaim to us both words of warning and words of God's steadfast, forgiving love.

CLOSING PRAYER: Our Father: We are thankful that you have given us the Ten Commandments and other teachings to help guide our lives. Sometimes we don't follow your way any better than the early Israelites. From time to time, we fail. We know, however, that you love us, forgive us, and will restore us to an eternal relationship with you. Send your Holy Spirit to sustain us and guide us in your way. In Jesus' name we pray. Amen.

Questions for Reflection or Discussion:

1. Imagine that you are standing at the foot of Mt. Sinai when God comes down and speaks like thunder out of the fire and smoke. What do you think? How do you feel? What do you do? Have you, or anyone you know, ever had even a remotely similar experience?

2. Which of the Ten Commandments (Exodus 20:1-17) do you think is the easiest to obey? Which is the easiest to break? Why?

3. The Covenant requires worshiping only the God of the Bible and following all his teachings. What are our false gods, our idols? Which of God's teachings, besides those of the Ten Commandments, are we most apt to neglect or disobey?

4. Are there any modern-day prophets (men or women) who both warn of the consequences of our individual and social behaviors, and also promise the gift of God's forgiving love if we return to him and his ways? Who are they? Are they persecuted? If not, are they really proclaiming *all* of God's Word?

5. Jesus mentioned some of the Ten Commandments in his Sermon on the Mount. (**Read Matthew 5:21-24, 27-30, 33-37.**) Jesus requires more of us than do the original Commandments. He seems to be concerned about our inner attitudes, as well as our outward actions. What do you think of Jesus' new requirements?

15
Amos
Prophet of Judgment

Amos 1, 2, 4, 5, 9

OPENING PRAYER: Eternal God, you are the LORD of all places and all seasons. Spring is a time of birth, of growth, of plans for the future. The rain and warmth of summer is a time for cultivating old and new plantings, a time to mature. The cool of autumn, after the work of harvest, is a time for slowing down, a time to prepare for the coming winter. Winter is a time of cold, a time for rest, a time for death. In your plan, spring *always* follows winter. Spring brings *new* life, abundant eternal life with you. For all the seasons of our lives, we give you thanks. Each season is a time for hope, a time for looking forward to the next stage in your gift of life. We are especially thankful for your gift of life and love and hope in Jesus Christ, who taught us to pray together, saying The Lord's Prayer . . . .

LESSON: We continue our study of Old Testament prophets. Amos was the first of the eighth century B.C. prophets. He was a rough, straight-talking herdsman from the edge of the desert. He came into town preaching words of judgment. But he also told of the promise of God's love. He spoke to the people and the conditions of his time and place. Where did he preach, and what was happening in his time?

When Solomon died, the large, powerful kingdom that he and his father, David, had built fell apart. The northern part was called Israel. The smaller southern part, which included Jerusalem, was called Judah. Jereboam the Second was king of Israel. The country was prosperous—for the upper class. The rich had become richer, while the poor had lost their land and were in debt to the rich. The priests didn't question these conditions.

They celebrated the religious festivals and ignored the mistreatment of the poor.

One day Amos showed up at a large religious gathering and gave the word of God's judgment to the king, queen, priests, and people.

He began: "Thus says the LORD: For three transgressions of Damascus, and for four, I will not revoke the punishment" (1:3). Amos went on to spell out what Syria, Israel's enemy, had done, and how God would punish them.

He continued: "Thus says the LORD: For three transgressions of Gaza, and for four, I will not revoke the punishment" (1:6). (The Philistines, also, had long been enemies of Israel and Judah.) One by one, Amos pronounced judgment on other nations the people of Israel considered enemies. By the time he came to Tyre and Moab, the people were saying "Amen" to each word of judgment.

Then he said, "Thus says the LORD: For three transgressions of Israel, and for four, I will not revoke the punishment" (2:6).

"Us? What have *we* done wrong?" the Israelites wondered.

Amos told them: "Because they sell [into slavery] the righteous for silver, and the needy for a pair of sandals . . . and push the afflicted out of the way; father and son go in to the same [slave] girl . . . and in the house of their God, they drink wine bought with fines they imposed. . . . [A]nd commanded the prophets, saying, 'You shall not prophesy'" (2:6-8, 12). Later he said, "They do not know how to do right, says the LORD" (3:10).

Then Amos turned to the Queen and rich ladies with her and said, "Listen to this, you women of Samaria, who grow fat like the well-fed cows of Bashan, who mistreat the weak, oppress the poor, and demand that your husbands keep you supplied with liquor!" (4:1 GNB). And Amos described the troubles that would result.

They protested, "But we worship the LORD regularly!"

God, speaking through Amos, told them: "I hate, I despise your festivals, and I take no delight in your solemn assemblies. Even though you offer me your burnt offerings and grain offerings, I will not accept them. . . . I will not listen to the melodies of your harps. But let justice roll down like waters, and righteousness like an everflowing stream" (5:21-24).

These words are just a sample of Amos's judgment message. He also brought some words of promise: "Thus says the LORD . . . Seek me and live . . . Seek good and not evil, that you may live; and so the LORD, the God of hosts, will be with you. . . . The time is surely coming, says the LORD . . . I will restore the fortunes of my people Israel . . . I will plant them upon their land . . . the land that I have given them, says the LORD your God" (5:4, 14; 9:13-15).

After Amos's words of judgment, I wonder if anyone stayed to hear his words of promise? Jewish legend holds that they stuffed him in a log and sawed the log in two! They had put their faith in other gods, in economic success, and in empty religious ceremonies—not in justice and righteousness.

CLOSING PRAYER: O God, our Father: We are thankful for your Word that comes to us through the words of Amos. You tell us that even when the words of judgment are loud in our ears, there is still your word of promise. You love us and forgive us. You stand at the door with open arms, waiting for us to come home. Thank you, LORD. Amen.

Questions for Reflection or Discussion

1. If a prophet like Amos were sent by God today, what might he or she say to us about other nations of the world? What words of judgment might we hear about our own society?
2. If the message carried the *spirit* of Jesus, what specific behaviors might be criticized in our families? Our economy? Our community? Our churches?
3. Could you "speak for God" about any issues in our country? What issues? What would you say? Would it reflect the concern of the prophets for the poor and disadvantaged? Would it reflect the loving concern of Jesus?
4. Apply Amos's word of promise to your personal life and behavior. Are there things you would have to stop "seeking"? What new goals should you now "seek"? How would you feel, and how would you respond to God's promised presence among us?

16
Hosea
Prophet of Forgiving Love

Hosea 1:1-11; 2:1-23; 3:1-5; 11:1-9

OPENING PRAYER: We are thankful, Father, for your many gifts. Ever since we were children, you have stood by us, ready to support us. Now that we are old, we need you even more. We need you to be with us in our troubles, our loneliness, our pain. Through the years, we have learned that you are always with us; your arms are always reaching out to hold us close. We are thankful for the loving forgiveness you show to all your children. We are grateful for love in the family—the love of parents and children, of husbands and wives, of friends. We are most thankful, Father, for your gift of salvation through the love of your Son Jesus Christ, in whose name we pray, using the words he taught us, saying The Lord's Prayer . . . .

LESSON: We continue to study the prophets whom God called to speak his Word to Israel and Judah in the eighth century B.C. They also have a message for us, for today. Hosea, like Amos, also preached to Israel. He warned his people of the trouble they were creating for themselves, but he also emphasized the God *he* knew, a God of love and forgiveness.

(Read Hosea 1:1-11.) Hosea is a hard book to read and understand, but a very interesting one. We can learn a lot from it. It presents God's relationship with his people in terms of family relationships. First, God is the "husband" and Israel his "wife." Later in the book, God speaks with great tenderness to Israel, as a father to his son.

Difficulty arises when the description of Hosea's relationship with Gomer, his wife, is confused with God's relationship to

Israel. It is hard to tell when Hosea is speaking to or about Gomer, and when he is bringing God's message to God's "wife," Israel. The account skips back and forth.

One thing is clear, however: Both "wives" are unfaithful. Gomer ran off with other men; she even became a prostitute. Israel worshiped and sacrificed to other gods. It was out of these experiences that Hosea learned about love and forgiveness, both divine and human. He discovered that he, a mere human being, had some capacity for forgiveness. This gave him insight into God's feelings for Israel.

Let us explore selected verses that communicate the Word of God which comes to us from this ancient prophet.

Hosea and Gomer had three children, and he spoke first to them about himself and their mother: "My children, plead with your mother—though she is no longer a wife to me, and I am no longer her husband. Plead with her to stop her adultery and prostitution. . . . She herself said, 'I will go to my lovers—they give me food and water, wool and linen, olive oil and wine'" (2:2, 5 GNB). Then, without a break, the passage becomes God speaking to Israel as *his* unfaithful "wife." The people had come to believe that false gods—in particular, the Baals—provided them with food and life's other necessities.

They believed that if you sacrificed to them, they would make wheat grow, olive trees bear fruit, and sheep and cattle bear lots of young.

"[Israel] would never acknowledge that I am the one who gave her the grain, the wine, the olive oil, and all the silver and gold that she used in the worship of Baal. So at harvest time I will take back my gifts of grain and wine, and will take away the wool and the linen I gave her for clothing. I will strip her naked in front of her lovers . . . I will put an end to all her festivities . . . all her religious meetings. I will destroy her grapevines and her fig trees, which she said her lovers gave her for serving them. . . . I will punish her for the times that she forgot me, when she burned incense to Baal and put on her jewelry to go chasing after her lovers. The LORD has spoken" (2:8-13 GNB).

That was God's indictment, his word of judgment which Hosea brought to the people.

However, the word of promise follows immediately: "Israel, I will make you my wife [again, that is]; I will be true and faithful; I will show you constant love and mercy and make you mine forever. I will keep my promise and make you mine, and you will acknowledge me as LORD. At that time I will answer the prayers of my people Israel. I will make rain fall on the earth, and the earth will produce grain and grapes and olives. I will establish my people in the land and make them prosper" (2:19-23 GNB).

God led Hosea to see that his marriage vows were like the covenant between God and his people; that his marriage relationship was like that between God and his people Israel. When Gomer first left him, he was hurt and angry. He planned a way to catch and punish her. He spoke the word of judgment to her as God did to Israel.

However, with God's help, he came to feel and to speak a word of love and forgiveness: "The LORD said to me, 'Go again and show your love for a woman who is committing adultery. . . . You must love her just as I still love the people of Israel, even though they turn to other gods and like to make offerings . . . to idols.' So I paid fifteen pieces of silver and seven bushels of barley to buy her. I told her that for a long time she would have to wait for me without being a prostitute or committing adultery; and during this time I would wait for her" (3:1-3 GNB).

Did you notice the words "go again"? Scholars take this, and other passages, to mean that Hosea forgave his unfaithful wife at least twice. We know that God forgave Israel (and Judah) *many* times. In any case, the power of God's love grew in Hosea until he was able to forgive, love, and take back his unfaithful wife.

We close with a beautiful passage in which God speaks to Israel like a father to his child: "The LORD says, 'When Israel was a child, I loved him and called him out of Egypt as my son. But the more I called to him, the more he turned away from me. My people sacrificed to Baal; they burned incense to idols. Yet I was the one who taught Israel to walk. I took my people up in my arms, but they did not acknowledge that I took care of them. I drew them to me with affection and love. I picked them up and held them to my cheek; I bent down to them and fed them.

[Yet] they refuse to return to me. . . . They insist on turning away from me. . . . [Nevertheless] how can I give you up, Israel? How can I abandon you? . . . My heart will not let me do it! My love for you is too strong. I will not punish you in my anger; I will not destroy Israel again. For I am God and not man. I, the Holy One, am with you. I will not come to you in anger'" (11:1-5, 7-9 GNB).

What a beautiful expression of God's love! He is a parent who picks up his child who has fallen and is hurt. In affection and love, he holds the child tenderly against his cheek. Even when the child insists on running away, he cannot give him up. That is what God, our Heavenly Father, is like.

There is another word for us here; a reminder that you and I are created in the Divine image. God loves and forgives; Hosea loved and forgave; so can we.

CLOSING PRAYER: Father: We are thankful for both the divine love and the human love revealed to us by your prophet Hosea. You love us too much to come to us in anger. Instead, you forgive us. Tenderly, you reach down to care for us and hold us close. And we are thankful. We are thankful also that, created in your image, we too can love and forgive others. Send your Holy Spirit to help us. We ask this in the spirit of Jesus. Amen.

Questions for Reflection or Discussion

1. Do these Scriptures convince you that God forgives us again and again? Why or why not?
2. What word, phrase, or sentence in Hosea's words from God is most comforting to you? Why?
3. Do you believe that *all* human beings, created in the image of God, are capable of forgiving others who have hurt them terribly? Why or why not?
4. Have you ever seen examples of forgiving love toward a husband or wife, a parent or child, like that of Hosea to Gomer or of God to Israel? Describe.
5. Are you able to forgive people who hurt you?

17
Jeremiah
Judgment and Promise

Jeremiah 1:4-10; 7:5-15; 31:31-34; Lamentations 3:20-33

OPENING PRAYER: O God, Father of our Lord Jesus Christ: You are our strength and shield, our ever-present help in time of trouble. We have good times and bad times, but you are present with us all the time. When our lives are smooth and happy, help us to be aware of your presence and be thankful, giving you praise for your love and care. When the going gets rough, O LORD, help us to lean back on your ever-lasting arms, being sure that you will carry us through troubled waters into the promised land of eternal life with you. Loving God, we pray to you in the words your Son Jesus taught us, saying together The Lord's Prayer . . . .

LESSON: We continue to study the prophets whom God called to speak to Israel and Judah, from about 750 B.C. until after the fall of Jerusalem in 596 B.C. God called many kinds of people to be prophets. Among the eighth-century prophets, Amos was a tough-talking herdsman. Hosea was a husband who forgave his unfaithful wife. Isaiah was an upper-class, well-informed high official in Judah. Jeremiah, the subject of this lesson, was a mere teenager. He was fifteen or sixteen when God called him to speak to a sick society. Here is how he reported it. (**Read Jeremiah 1:4-10.**)

About one hundred years before Jeremiah's time, Israel had been conquered, as Amos had threatened. Now Judah was also breaking the Covenant. Jeremiah prophesied to Judah and nearby nations from about 626 B.C. to the fall of Jerusalem in 596 B.C., and for ten years after Judah fell. Here is part of a sermon preached by Jeremiah in the Temple itself. First he delivered

God's word of promise, and then God's word of judgment. **(Read Jeremiah 7:5-15.)**

During his career, Jeremiah was in and out of trouble. When the Babylonian army surrounded Jerusalem, he advised the king to surrender and ask God's forgiveness for breaking the Covenant. The king threw Jeremiah into an empty cistern in the palace courtyard. He was up to his waist in mud (see Jeremiah 38:1-13). An Ethiopian servant of the king interceded for Jeremiah. He was pulled out, but kept under house arrest. Being a faithful prophet was not an easy—or safe—job!

We conclude with two examples of God's word of promise. The first, proclaimed by Jeremiah, has long been read by Christians as foreseeing the covenant community God created through Jesus, the Church of which you and I are members. **(Read Jeremiah 31:31-34.)**

The second is found in the book of Lamentations, written after the destruction of Jerusalem. Its poet author is in despair, in the midst of the death, hunger, and destruction. He writes that it is as if his face had been ground down into the dirt until his teeth were broken on gravel.

Yet even then, he speaks God's word of hope, promise, and love: "My spirit is depressed, yet hope returns when I remember this one thing: The LORD's unfailing love and mercy still continue, fresh as the morning, sure as the sunrise. The LORD is all I have, and so in him I put my hope. The LORD is good to everyone who trusts in him, so it is best for us to wait in patience—to wait for him to save us. The LORD is merciful, and will not reject us forever. He may bring us sorrow, but His love for us is sure and strong. He takes no pleasure in causing us grief or pain" (3:20-24; 31-33; 25-26 GNB).

God loves us and forgives us. That's the Good News of the Bible, revealed most completely in the saving, suffering love of Jesus.

CLOSING PRAYER: Father: Like Jeremiah and all the prophets, we too know suffering, loss, pain, despair. You are the Lord who is always present with us. There is joyful hope for us when we remember that your unfailing love and mercy still continue, new and fresh every day, as predictable as the sunrise. We put our trust in you and wait patiently for you to save us. For all this, and much more, we are thankful. Praise the LORD! Amen.

Questions for Reflection or Discussion

1. How old were you when you committed your life to God? Can you share your experience?
2. Do you believe that a teenager could bring God's message to his elders? Why or why not? Is there a "hint" here about the way we think about and react to our teenagers?
3. Are true prophets always disliked and usually persecuted? Why? Is there a "hint" here about our reaction to critics who "step on toes"? Is this why we hesitate to speak out for what we think is right?
4. What evidence have you seen, in your life or that of others, that God's unfailing love and mercy are as sure as the sunrise? Has that given you enough hope, so that you may be patient while waiting for God to act? Why or why not?

18
"You Are Forgiven; Come Home!"

Isaiah 40–44

OPENING PRAYER: Eternal God: Your Kingdom is from everlasting to everlasting. In the beginning, you created the earth, the sky, the sea. You created us; we are your children. We are thankful that we are precious in your sight, that you love us and take care of us. You do not remember our sins. When we faint, you renew our strength and bear us up in your everlasting arms. We pray that today, as we seek your Word in Scripture, you will send your Holy Spirit to renew our trust in you, and in Jesus Christ our Lord, who taught us to pray together, saying The Lord's Prayer . . . .

LESSON: Our study of the prophets moves to the Prophet of the Exile. We do not know his name. His sermons are chapters 40–55 in the book of Isaiah. They were placed there long ago, because his message is similar to that of Isaiah of Jerusalem.

Isaiah was one of the eighth century B.C. prophets whom God sent to call his people back to the Covenant. Only a few of the people listened and obeyed. Most continued to break the Covenant. So Israel was conquered by Assyria in 722 B.C. Its people were so scattered that they became the Lost Tribes of Israel. Judah survived another 135 years, until Babylon conquered it in 587 B.C. Its king, priests, and leading citizens were carried into exile, the Babylonian captivity. About fifty years later, God called the Prophet of the Exile.

The Prophet of the Exile preached the "good news" of God's forgiving love to God's chosen people, saying they would soon be allowed to go back to Jerusalem, to Zion. We can believe his words are addressed to us, too. In them, you can hear the Good

News of God's love for you, for you *personally*. There is a special word here for those who are old and tired, weak and worried, and sometimes afraid, even angry.

"I have swept away your transgressions like a cloud, and your sins like mist; return to me, for I have redeemed you" (44:22). To the people he had banished from Jerusalem for their sins, God did *not* say, "Come back, then I will forgive you." No! He told them, and he tells us, "Come back, I have already forgiven you." There are few words in the Bible that are better news than that.

(Read Isaiah 43:2-4; 40:28-31.) There are three things to note about these passages. First, as we noted in an earlier lesson, the LORD, written in capital letters is substituted for the holy personal name which God revealed to Moses from the burning bush, revealed so that we can have a personal relationship with him.

Second, when Isaiah says "wait for the LORD" (40:31), he means "trust God," depend on him. Do not be anxious. Be patient; give God time to work things out for you.

Third, this is poetry: "Mount up with wings like eagles . . . run and not be weary" (v. 31). When we are old, our running and flying days are usually over—physically. However, these words can refer to our inner selves, our spiritual lives. When we patiently trust in the LORD, we can expect our inner lives to be revived, renewed, so that our spirits can soar, as we wait for that "great gittin' up morning."

One final word from this prophet of long ago, a word for us today: "I am the first and I am the last; besides me there is no god. . . . Do not fear, or be afraid; have I not told you from of old and declared it? . . . Is there any god besides me? There is no other rock; I know not one" (44:6c, 8).

This is indeed good news: those who trust God "shall renew their [inner] strength"; their spirits will soar up to God as on eagles' wings. For the LORD our God is the *only* Rock, the firm foundation of our salvation.

CLOSING PRAYER: O God, who loves and forgives us: You are the rock to which we cling, on which we stand; the Lord in whom we trust. We seldom run anymore. We are often faint and weary, but we need not be afraid. We look forward with hope to the day when we will join you in your heavenly Kingdom. Thank you, LORD. Amen.

Questions for Reflection or Discussion

1. Can you really believe that God says to wandering sons and daughters, "Come on home, I have already forgiven you"? Does this remind you of a parable Jesus told? (See Luke 15:11-20.)

2. Is it significant that the Exiles heard that word of promise after fifty years of captivity, and the Prodigal Son after waking up in a pigpen? Do we have to "hit bottom" before we listen to God? What can we do to hear God earlier?

3. Describe your experiences, or those of someone you know well, of "passing through troubled waters" or "walking through fire." What evidence did you see that God was there with you?

4. Describe your experiences, or those of someone you know well, of mounting up on eagle wings, or of feeling that your strength is renewed. Do you feel secure on the solid Rock of God's love?

19
Meeting God Face to Face

Public Worship, a Drama in Three Acts

Isaiah 6:1-9a

OPENING PRAYER: Our Father in Heaven: You are high and lifted up, beyond our grasp and understanding. Yet you are also right here with us, closer than hands and feet. We have felt your love and care. You hear us when we pray; when we open up the desires and fears of our hearts, you come to help us. In Christ, you have made us brothers and sisters, and you have instructed us to love one another as you have loved us. As your children, we gather to be aware of your Presence and to listen for the Word you speak to each of us. Send your Holy Spirit to help us truly pray the words your Son Jesus Christ, our Lord, taught us, saying The Lord's Prayer . . . .

LESSON: Our religion has two aspects or dimensions. One is our personal relationship with the creating God who gave us his holy personal name. This is a *vertical* relationship, between us and the God who is high and lifted up. Then there is our relationship with other persons, a *horizontal* one with fellow human beings. When we experience God's love, it flows through us in love and service to others. These two relationships, with God and with one another, are combined in the life of the Church. God has called us together in the Church to be brothers and sisters in Christ.

Prayer and worship are at the center of the Christian life. When we think of prayer, most of us think of our individual, personal conversation with God. Prayer also can be a group activity, as when we pray together in worship. In worship, we gather in God's presence as a community of faith, to tell and retell the old,

old story of our human experience with the creating, nurturing, instructing, loving, and forgiving God, revealed in Scripture and God's Son, Jesus Christ.

This lesson's focus is on public worship, the service of praise and thanksgiving which, as a group, we offer to God. What goes on in a service of worship? What *should* go on? What are we supposed to do, think, and feel during worship? Actually, there are many forms of Christian worship, ranging from the silence and spontaneous speech of Quakers to the formal ritual of the Mass. However, in one way or another, most contain the same basic elements. These elements are revealed in the sixth chapter of Isaiah, where the prophet describes his dramatic encounter with God. To get its full meaning, we need to know who Isaiah was, and where he was when he heard God call him to be a prophet.

Isaiah was in the Temple in Jerusalem during a special once-a-year ceremony. Priests, king, and people had gathered to welcome and celebrate the LORD's presence among his chosen people. God's presence in the Temple was symbolized by the Ark of the Covenant in the Holy of Holies, a room behind the altar for sacrifices. Very few persons could enter there, and then only after prayerful preparation, which included a time of chaste moral behavior followed by ritual cleansing. Those who had not undergone this preparation—including priests, king, and nobles—had to stay outside the doors. Yet Isaiah was inside. Was he a priest? A member of the royal family? We do not know. Nevertheless, he had prepared, and had *thought* he was worthy to be in God's presence.

(Read Isaiah 6:1-9a.) This account of Isaiah's face-to-face meeting with God can be understood as a drama in three acts, providing an outline of what happens when we worship.

Act One in the drama of worship begins when we meet God, when we are aware of his presence. Awareness of God's presence has three results:

1. We experience God in all his majesty and power, his glory spreading throughout all creation. In other words, we experience the most ultimate reality in the universe. Any part of the service may evoke this experience: Scripture, music, sermon, prayer,

silence. In fact, it can happen at any place, at any time. God is everywhere.

2. When we become aware of God, we see ourselves clearly. Like Isaiah, we come to realize that we are unworthy to be in God's presence. We have fallen short of his expectations. We feel embarrassed, ashamed. We confess that both we and our society have failed to live up to the Divine standard.

3. When we confess, the miracle of God's love occurs—again! It burns and cleanses like fire. We experience forgiveness; we accept forgiveness.

When we truly meet God, we learn that, yes, we are sinners, but we are *forgiven* sinners. That is the Good News of the gospel. God loves us; we are his children.

The *Second Act* in the drama of worship is made possible by that experience of and acceptance of forgiveness:

1. When we realize our unworthiness and confess it, then and only then do we hear the Word God speaks. God's forgiving love cleanses and opens our ears, our mind, and our heart, so that we can hear God's special word for us. That word is often, as it was for Isaiah, a call, something for you and me to be and to do. The call may be a word to say or an act of love to perform toward someone who needs it, whether that person be family, friend, or stranger. At other times, the word is one of comfort and hope: God saying, "I love you. I will take care of you."

2. Having heard that Word, like Isaiah, we face a moment of decision. Will I accept it, act on it, live by it? Will I do what God asks? Will I make the change in my thought and behavior that God wants? Will I stop worrying; cease to be afraid and trust him; put my life—and my death—into his hands? God does not make us do anything. He gave us free will, so we can, and must, decide.

3. The climax of worship is when we decide to say "Yes" to God and to his Word: "Yes, LORD; here I am; I will do as you say."

The *Third* and final *Act* of worship is short, and can be wonderfully sweet. In worship, as in all of life, God has the last word.

That word is "Go!" He sends us away from the place of worship, back into the world of everyday life. We are sent with the reassurance that God loves us and goes with us. The Church calls this "sending forth" the benediction, which means "good word." And it *is* good! It is God's promise that, as the Holy Spirit, he goes with us, that his love is with us through thick and thin. All through life, and also in death, God is with us; we are not alone. He is right here, leading and sustaining us until we join him in his heavenly home.

CLOSING PRAYER: God and Father of us all: We are your children, and we are thankful that we can have a close personal relationship with you. We are also thankful that we can share your Presence with others in public worship. We pray that we may experience your love, hear your voice, and go on with our lives confident that you are with us all the way. Thank you, LORD. Amen.

Questions for Reflection or Discussion

1. Describe a time when you were aware of God's presence. Was it during private prayer or public worship? Is it easier for you to feel close to God during private devotions or public worship? Why?
2. During such times, to what extent and in what ways are your experiences similar to or different from those of Isaiah?
3. During such experiences, what do you hear God saying to you? If a "call," to what? If a word of comfort, how do you respond?
4. What aspect or part of public worship most helps you to be aware of God and to hear his word for you? Why?

Part II
THE NEW TESTAMENT

THE LONG-EXPECTED JESUS

20

Messiah Is Coming: Get Ready

Mark 1:1-8; Isaiah 9:2, 6-7

OPENING PRAYER: Gracious God: Help us to know you better, so that we can love you more. We know you as the Creator, giver of life; as the Holy Spirit, our guide and comforter; as Jesus, the Son, God with us, our Savior and friend. We are thankful for all these ways you reveal yourself to us. We are particularly grateful for the revelation of your saving love through Jesus. Send your Holy Spirit to help us study and thus understand better what the birth, ministry, and death of Jesus means for us and for all humankind. Help us to pray, using the words he taught us, saying The Lord's Prayer . . . .

LESSON: With this lesson, our Bible study moves from the Old to the New Testament. Both bear witness to God's mighty works in our world, and to the steadfast love with which he calls every human being into relationship with him. The Old Testament concentrates on God's relationship with the children of Israel. Its enduring message of God's majesty and steadfast love is told powerfully by the prophets and psalmists. It was the Scripture that Jesus knew and loved; it is our Scripture, too.

Our study of the New Testament begins with Jesus. The lessons in Part II follow his life from birth through his ministry and teachings, his death and resurrection, to the Church created to continue his saving work. This lesson is the first of five through which we try to understand the meaning of Jesus' birth as the "advent," the coming of Divine Love into human existence. It came in the form of a Jewish baby, born in a Bethlehem stable. What does that mean for us?

Jesus' birth means that God came into our world as a baby called Emmanuel, which is Hebrew for "God with us." John's Gospel says that "the Word [of God] became flesh and dwelt among us" (1:14 KJV). Divinity came into human life as a helpless baby, to share our life from birth through death, to feel what we feel, to identify with us, to be the model for our lives, to love us enough to die for our salvation.

Both Old and New Testaments speak of the One to come. The prophets told of God's promise of a future time, when sins would be forgiven and life would be secure and peaceful. Jesus' disciples, believing him to be the Messiah, thought that blessed time had come. Thus they were puzzled by his cruel death: How could the Son of Man, who came to save Israel, die, leaving all the old powers in control? The empty tomb lifted their sadness, but left them wondering about who and what Jesus really was. They turned to their Scripture, seeking answers; and they found them, especially in the writing of the prophets. They found words which they accepted as an explanation, words that most Christians still accept as a forecast of Jesus' birth and of his saving ministry. Among the best known is Isaiah 9:2, 6-7. (**Read Isaiah 9:2, 6-7.**)

The New Testament has more direct announcements of Jesus' imminent coming. One Gospel begins with this almost breathless proclamation. (**Read Mark 1:1-8.**)

Scripture tells us, "He is coming; get ready!" We, too, can look forward to "the long-expected Jesus." To be ready to receive him, we need to look into our minds and hearts. What do we need to change, to get rid of, so that we will be ready to receive him fully, joyfully? The study of Jesus' birth is a way we can prepare to refill our hearts and minds with God's love, born that first Christmas. God comes to us in Jesus Christ *every* Christmas. He comes *every day* into our hearts and minds, if we are prepared to receive him. He's coming; no doubt about it. Get ready!

CLOSING PRAYER: We are thankful, Father, that you came into our lives in Jesus. He came to share our humanness, our experiences in life and in death. He loved us enough to die, painfully, to save us. He came; he is always coming, every Christmas, every day. Praise the LORD. Amen.

Questions for Reflection or Discussion

1. The Church calls the weeks before Christmas "Advent," a time to prepare for the "coming" of God into our world as a human baby. Do we really need to "get ready" for Jesus? Why? When? How?
2. Whether we get ready to receive Jesus once a year, once a week, or daily, exactly what helps us to be ready for Jesus' entry into our hearts? That is, what thoughts and behaviors are involved in "expecting" and "preparing"?
3. What old thoughts, behaviors, and habits do you need to discard, and what new ones do you need to acquire in order to receive Jesus more fully and joyfully?
4. What does Jesus' coming, his living and dying, tell us about the faithfulness with which God keeps his promises?

21
God Prepares
a Way in the Desert

Luke 1:26-33; Isaiah 35:1-10

OPENING PRAYER: Heavenly Father, father of our Lord Jesus Christ: We are thankful that you gave us, on that first Christmas Day, your divine presence and love in the Babe of Bethlehem. We look forward to next Christmas, when again we will celebrate his birth. His life gives us life. His death saved us from the death of sin. Help us get ready to receive again this great gift of your saving love in Christ Jesus. Remembering him, we pray together using the words he taught us, saying The Lord's Prayer . . . .

LESSON: We are attempting to understand the meaning of Jesus' birth, ministry, and death. Usually, we get ready for Christmas by decorating trees, cooking turkey, and rushing around shopping malls. Is there a better way to prepare for the birth of Jesus, God coming into our world in human form?

Old Testament passages speak of One who will come. In the New Testament, we read announcements that he is just about to arrive. We begin with the angel's report to Mary. (**Read Luke 1:26-33.**)

"Of his kingdom there will be no end" (Luke 1:33). You can imagine the wonder and expectation this message awakened in Mary's mind and heart. Of course she did not yet know that this new human life would begin in a barn and end on a Cross.

About 600 years before the angel's message to Mary, God spoke to the children of Israel through a prophet. He promised that, scattered by war and famine into distant lands, they would return home to Jerusalem. It would be a hard journey through the desert, but they would have God's help. After Jesus died, his disciples understood this passage to refer to Jesus and his ministry. So the following words came first to those early children of Israel; then to Jesus' bereaved disciples; and now to us. These words speak of the joy, expectation, and hope of a Way, a road to some promised future. Even though it runs through wilderness, our journey is made possible by God acting in Jesus. **(Read Isaiah 35:1-10.)**

This Scripture is gospel! The old English word "gospel" can mean both "God-speak" (i.e., what God has said) and also "good news," "glad tidings." What God speaks *is* Good News! These comforting words say to us, perhaps especially to those of us who are old, worried, tired, perhaps afraid: "Be strong; fear not: behold, your God will come . . . he will come and save you" (35:4 KJV).

That is the message of Jesus' birth. It is the Christmas hope and expectation that can give new strength to tired hands and knees (and minds!) that tremble. It is the hope, the joy, the security that the birth of Jesus promises. He prepared the way to eternal abundant life in Heaven. "Be strong, fear not!" We can, and should, believe this ancient promise of the Good News. Thanks be to God!

CLOSING PRAYER: Eternal, creating God: You created us in your own image. In Jesus, you saved us for eternal life with you. He shows us the Way into that life. Help us to follow him, faithfully and bravely. This we ask in Jesus' name. Amen.

Questions for Reflection or Discussion

1. Try to identify with Mary. What was she expecting? How did she feel? What special preparations did she make? Would you have said "Yes" to God?
2. The angel said, "Of his kingdom there will be no end." What do you understand that statement to mean?
3. Jesus shows us the way into abundant life with God. Does it go through a wilderness? What desolate places have you gone through? How has God "strengthened weak hands and feeble knees"? How has he made "sorrow and sighing flee away"?
4. Is it difficult or easy for you to "Be strong, fear not; your God will come and save you"? Why? In what ways?

22
God Offers a New Covenant

Matthew 1:18-21; Jeremiah 31:31-34; Isaiah 28:16

OPENING PRAYER: Eternal God, our Father: Be with us as we think about Christmas and what Christ's coming means. We look forward to celebrating the birth of Jesus, our Christ, your Son. In him, your forgiving love was revealed most completely. We are thankful. Send your Holy Spirit; help us understand this gift, and accept more completely our freedom from sin, which enables us to receive new, abundant, eternal life with you. We ask this in Jesus' name, who taught us to pray together, saying The Lord's Prayer . . . .

LESSON: The long-expected birth of Jesus represented Divinity's entrance into our world as a living, breathing human baby. In Jesus, God came to us. He came to share our humanness, to understand us, to identify with us. He came to save us from sin. That is what Christmas is all about, not presents under a decorated tree and turkey with dressing. It is Jesus' birthday. Therefore, the best way to get ready is not by shopping or cooking, but by preparing to accept Jesus into our lives more completely than ever before.

Both Old and New Testaments help us do just that. We will study three statements about the meaning of Jesus' birth, life, and death. The first is an angel's message in Joseph's dream about Mary and the baby she was expecting: "The child conceived in her is from the Holy Spirit. She will bear a son, and you are to name him Jesus, for he will save his people from their sins" (Matthew 1:20-21). Jesus was God in human flesh, revealing divine forgiving love for all his people, saving *us* from our sins. That is the central meaning of Christmas. That is Good News!

Long before Jesus' birth, Jeremiah spoke of something new that God would do, someday when the time was right. (**Read**

Jeremiah 31:31-34.) We are people of this New Covenant. During the Last Supper, Jesus said that the wine of Holy Communion represents "the new covenant in my blood" (Luke 20:20), poured out for the forgiveness of sin. In accepting Jesus' gift from the cross, we accept God's love and teachings within us, written on our hearts. That is part of the Good News of Christmas.

Isaiah also spoke of what God was planning. His society, like ours, was troubled and confused; the people trusted in false ideas and worshiped false gods. Here is what Isaiah told his people: "Thus says the LORD GOD: 'Behold, I am laying in Zion for a foundation a Stone, a tested Stone, a precious cornerstone of sure foundation; [and on it is written] He who trusts in that Stone will not panic'" (Isaiah 28:16 TAB). For us, Jesus is that Rock. Trusting in that foundation, we can live and die, confident in God's love. When our faith in him is firm, we are secure. We can be calm, patient, waiting for God to act.

That is what Christmas, the birthday of Jesus, is all about: the Good News of God's grace, poured out for us, and for many. Praise the LORD!

CLOSING PRAYER: Heavenly Father: We thank you for Christmas; we thank you for Jesus. He is the solid rock laid as the foundation for our living, and for our dying. Trusting in you, we wait patiently for the gift of Christmas, the Baby Jesus who is also Christ our Savior. Amen.

Questions for Reflection or Discussion

1. Jesus' birthday, Christmas, is a very special day in the Christian Year. Last year, what did you do to get ready for Christmas? Do on Christmas Day? What changes, if any, should you make this year? Would that be hard or easy? Why?

2. In Luke, Mary is told that Jesus would be King of the house of Jacob. Matthew says Joseph was told that Jesus "will save his people from their sins." Which of these phrases best describes what Jesus did? Why?

3. Compare the Old Covenant [Exodus 19:5-6; 20:1-17] with Jeremiah's prediction of the New Covenant [Jeremiah 31:31-34]. In what ways are they alike and different? To what extent does the Church today fulfill Jeremiah's vision of the New Covenant?

23
Your God Is Coming!

Isaiah 40:1-11; James 5:7-11

OPENING PRAYER: Father, God: We give thanks to you for many things. Each of us, in his or her own heart, remembers gifts we have received from you. We have had bad times, too—hard days and nights. However, you are with us all the time. Your everlasting arms uphold us through everything; and we are thankful. We are especially thankful for the gift of your Son, our Savior, Jesus Christ. We look forward to his coming at Christmas, when we celebrate his birth. Help us get ready to accept him more completely into our minds and hearts. Thinking of him, we pray the prayer he taught us, saying together The Lord's Prayer . . . .

LESSON: This lesson concludes our attempt to understand Jesus' birth, to know the true meaning of Christmas. As Christians, what we expect at Christmas is not Santa Claus or a tree with presents under it. We look forward to celebrating again the birth of Jesus, the Savior who loves us and takes care of us. So our "expecting" is for holy and spiritual things. Our preparations, too, should be spiritual, preparing our minds and hearts to receive the One who is always coming into hearts ready to receive him.

Many Old and New Testament Scriptures tell of Christ's coming. Previous lessons studied several of those. Now we focus on Isaiah 40:1-11. It contains a Word from God to the Babylonian exiles, who had spent two generations as captives in a foreign land.

The Prophet of the Exile tells them: God has forgiven you; your punishment is over; you soon will be going home to Jerusalem. " 'Comfort my people,' says our God. 'Comfort them! Encourage the people of Jerusalem. Tell them they have suffered long enough and their sins are now forgiven. I have punished them in full for all their sins' " (40:1-2 GNB).

God sent that happy news long before Jesus was born. Much later, after Jesus' death, his grieving disciples believed these words were addressed to them. They believed that this had already happened in the birth, life, death, and resurrection of Jesus.

The prophet's message continues: "Proclaim that all mankind are like grass; they last no longer than wild flowers. . . . Yes, grass withers and flowers fade, but the word of our God endures forever" (40:6, 8 GNB). Our lives are short. We are fragile, temporary. God, however, is from everlasting to everlasting. His love incarnate in Jesus Christ, his grace, and his power for salvation "endure forever."

The message from God continues: "Get you up on a high mountain, O Zion, herald of good tidings; lift up your voice with strength . . . say to the cities of Judah, 'Here is your God!' See, the Lord GOD comes with might . . . he will feed his flock like a shepherd; he will gather the lambs in his arms, and carry them in his bosom, and gently lead the mother sheep" (40:9-11).

The great old hymn, "Sing Praise to God," says, "As with a mother's tender hand, God gently leads the chosen band. To God all praise and glory." What the prophet spoke, Jesus illustrated: that God's loving care is for all his children, especially those most in need of help—the young lambs, those now weak and feeble.

This is the Bible's Good News for all God's children. It was good news to the Babylonian exiles, more than 500 years before Jesus was born. It was joyful news for Jesus' disciples, as they tried to understand the meaning of his physical death on the Cross. And it is good news for us. It helps us understand the importance and the joy of the birth of Mary's baby, Jesus, whom we call Savior. Jesus' birth means that God came into the world in human form to be with us. Suffering and dying, he revealed the Divine nature of a God who loves and saves—*everyone*.

So at Christmas, and every day of the year, we look for the God who comes to be with us; who came long ago to a stable in Bethlehem; who comes back every Christmas; who comes every day to those ready to receive him, to lead us into the Kingdom of

God. When will that be? We do not know, but we can look forward in hope, trusting in the grace of God. The Epistle of James advises us to wait patiently: "Be patient, then, my brothers until the Lord comes. See how patient a farmer is as he waits for his land to produce precious crops. . . . You also must be patient. Keep your hopes high, for the day of the Lord's coming is near. . . . For the Lord is full of mercy and compassion" (James 5:7, 8, 11*c* GNB).

CLOSING PRAYER: Dear loving Father: We are thankful for the gift of yourself in Jesus. Help us every day, and especially at Christmas, to be ready to receive him again into our lives; to receive both his comforting humanity and his powerful divine love. In the name of the Father, Son, and Holy Spirit. Amen.

Questions for Reflection or Discussion

1. What gives you hope when you feel as weak and temporary as grass?
2. Pick out the specific words in Isaiah 40:1-11 that comfort you the most. Why are they the most compelling?
3. Who first told you that *"Your* God is coming"? How was that message communicated? To whom have you carried that message, and how did you communicate it?
4. Is it difficult for you to wait, to be patient, as the Epistle of James advises? What helps you to wait patiently? What spiritual preparations will you make as you wait for the Savior to come this Christmas? To come today?

24
Christmas: He Is Here!

Luke 2:1-20; John 1:1-5, 14-18

OPENING PRAYER: Glory to God, our Father and the Father of Jesus Christ: We are thankful for all your many gifts to us. Your best gift came that first Christmas in Bethlehem. There your love was revealed in human form. It became flesh and dwelt among us: first in the baby Jesus; then in the preacher and healer who walked the roads of Galilee; and finally in the Savior who died on the cross to save us. We are thankful, Father, that you showed us your divine, everlasting love in a form we can understand, revealed in the man Jesus, whom we can know and love, and in the risen Christ, whom we can follow into eternal, abundant life with you. Thank you, LORD, for Christmas and all it means to us. As we remember Jesus, we pray together the prayer he taught us, saying The Lord's Prayer . . . .

LESSON: Christmas comes, as Jesus came and comes, whether we are ready or not. He is Emmanuel, God with us. That is the Doctrine of Incarnation: God in human form, in the flesh. Christmas emphasizes the humanness of Jesus. He is one of us. Born a human baby, he cried and laughed. He got hungry. He learned to walk and talk. He played. Jesus was, and is, human as we are. He also was, and is, divine. That is the mystery of Jesus the Christ, the complete uniting of divinity with humanity.

The Scriptures for this lesson are from the Gospels of Luke and John. Each introduces us to the Christmas event, God breaking into the world. Luke presents the human baby in a barn, yet surrounded by supernatural events. John presents him as the very essence of Divinity.

(**Read Luke 2:1-20.**) This was a human birth—a human mother and a human child. It occurred in a very humble place. The first people who knew about it were ordinary folks, shepherds. Yet, the event had divine implications. Angels sang "Glory to God," "Peace on Earth." Luke's account combines these human and divine aspects, the ordinary and the extraordinary. Maybe that is why Christmas is so exciting, so joyful. Maybe that explains why it is such Good News, even when it is a mystery we can never completely understand.

At Christmas we focus on the birth of the Babe of Bethlehem. That emphasizes the humanity of Jesus. He understands what it is like to be a human being. He knows the love of family and friends; good times at a wedding. He also knows sadness, being abandoned by family and friends. He knows what it is like to suffer and die. He understands us, loves us, takes care of us. He is our elder brother; he is our friend. We can feel close to him, follow him.

However, if we know only the baby Jesus, we miss two very important things that God did for us in Jesus Christ. First, that baby grew up to be a man who fully embodied God's nature and revealed it for all to see. Second, the mature Jesus died a painful death on a Cross for us.

Jesus was both a man and the Christ. John's Gospel tells us nothing at all about the human birth. It begins instead with emphasis on the Divine essence which became embodied in the flesh of a human being. (**Read John 1:1-5, 14-18.**)

The Bible is full of Good News, none of it better than the Christmas story. Through Jesus Christ, we can experience God. Through him we can know the hope of eternal life with God the Father, Son, and Holy Spirit.

CLOSING PRAYER: Gracious, loving God: We are thankful for the promise of that baby in the manger at Bethlehem. We are thankful for the Divine Word which became flesh to hang on the Cross, suffering and dying to give us eternal life with you. Glory to God in the highest, and on earth peace and goodwill to all men and women. Alleluia! Amen.

Questions for Reflection or Discussion

1. We meet Jesus first as a helpless baby. Think of all the ways the New Testament describes his human experiences— good, bad, happy, painful. What does the humanness of Jesus tell us about the nature of God? Does it help us to see and know him as Savior? As elder brother and friend?

2. How do John's words about the Word agree with, differ from, or complement Luke's picture? Which account helps you understand Jesus Christ better? Are both necessary?

3. Which aspect of Jesus Christ, his humanness or his divinity, do different denominations emphasize? Which is most important in your church? To you?

4. Which aspect of Jesus Christ (humanity or divinity) do most American Christians emphasize? Why do you think that is so? What are the good and bad results of each point of view?

5. Is there some more useful way of thinking about his fundamental nature? What?

25
Wise Men and a Star

Matthew 2:1-12

OPENING PRAYER: Father: Again we gather before you in Jesus' name. His star shone brightly in Bethlehem long ago. He is the Light of the World. We come again to seek your Word in Scripture. Help us to be aware of your Presence. Send your Holy Spirit to open our minds and hearts so that we can receive the light you have for each of us today. We ask this in the name of Jesus, the Babe in the manger and the Savior on the Cross, who taught us to pray together, saying The Lord's Prayer . . . .

LESSON: Jesus was a Jewish baby born in a stable in an obscure town of a small out-of-the-way country. Jews had long expected a messiah who would throw out the Roman army and restore the kingdom of David, so they could be free and prosperous again. Why do Christians believe that this Jesus was the Christ of all the world? The Bible's answer to that question begins with a visit from the Magi.

The story of Jesus' birth, especially as told by Luke, is very familiar to us. We know less about those visitors from the East and their significance. They came to Bethlehem *after* Christmas. The Church has called that day Epiphany, Greek for "to appear," as in a burst of light. The event shows that God revealed himself in Jesus Christ as a light shining on all his children.

(Read Matthew 2:1-5, 9-11.) Did you notice how this Bible account is different from the Christmas pageant performed in many churches? First, the "wisemen" were not in the stable with the shepherds, sheep, and cows on the night Jesus was born.

They came later, into a "house." Matthew does not say how many there were or what country they came from, or that they were kings. They were Magi—that is, learned scholars who studied the stars.

More important, they were foreigners, gentiles; not Jews. This shows that Jesus was not just the Jewish messiah. He came for everybody, everywhere. The star shone that night for everyone. God's love shines on all human beings. The Prophet of the Exile reports that God said, "I will also make you a light to the nations—so that all the world may be saved" (Isaiah 49:6 GNB).

The Gospel of John also refers to Jesus as light. Jesus said, "I am the light of the world" (John 8:12). You remember that John's Gospel begins by identifying Jesus as the Word. By "word," John meant the powerful creative revelation of God.

In the Bible's first chapter, we read that God *spoke* the world into existence, beginning with light: "Then God said, 'Let there be light'; and there was light. And God saw that the light was good" (Genesis 1:3-4a).

John wrote about Christ, that "[I]n him was life, and the life was the light of all people. The light shines in the darkness, and the darkness did not overcome it. . . . And the Word became flesh and lived among us . . . full of grace and truth. . . . From his fullness we have all received, grace upon grace" (John 1:4-5, 14, 16). This is the "amazing grace" we sing about, grace that brings hope and purpose to our lives.

The Star of Bethlehem is a light that shines on us, on all human beings. All we need to do is accept its warmth and brightness, even on our coldest and darkest days. The light of God's love shines every day for everyone, including you and me. It is a guiding star that can lead us, just as it led the Magi to Jesus Christ.

CLOSING PRAYER: Father: Our lives often seem cold and dark. Physical darkness and emotional darkness can create a valley of shadows through which we must walk. However, in Jesus, you are the Good Shepherd who goes with us, who leads us. O God, lift our eyes to Jesus. He is the light that leads us safely home to you. Thank you, LORD. Amen.

Questions for Reflection or Discussion

1. How does the idea of "Light" affect your understanding of Jesus, his ministry, and his relationship to you?
2. Is it easier to imagine yourself as a Shepherd or as a "wise man" coming to honor Jesus? Why?
3. After reading about the Magi, have you changed your ideas about who they were and what their significance is for our understanding of Jesus' birth and ministry? In what ways? Why?
4. John 1:4-5 says that Jesus is a light to all the world and the darkness has never put it out. To what extent does that describe the history of the Christian movement and the Church?
5. What types of darkness try to put out the Light of Christ? What can *you* do to help keep the Light shining for the world?

26
Manger Baby Becomes Messiah

Luke 2:41-52; Mark 1:9-11, 14-15

OPENING PRAYER: We are thankful, Father, for this new day. It is a time to study Scripture, to learn more about your Son Jesus Christ. Born a helpless baby long ago, he grew in wisdom and stature to become a strong Man for others, the Christ, our Savior. We are especially thankful, O LORD, for the forgiving love you poured out on us in his life, death, and resurrection. He taught us to pray saying The Lord's Prayer . . . .

LESSON: What does the Bible tell us about the life of Jesus, between the time he was born and when he began his very special mission about thirty years later? Not very much. In fact, the Gospels of Mark and John begin when Jesus is a grown man. Luke tells us a little, beginning with Jesus' visit to Jerusalem as a twelve-year-old boy.

(**Read Luke 2:41-52.**) At twelve, many Jewish boys had their Bar Mitzvah, a ceremony admitting them to adult status, including voting membership in a synagogue. Jesus was ready for these responsibilities. However, he did more than just listen; he asked questions. He amazed those who heard him, including his parents. He already felt a special relationship with God as his Father.

The Bible is almost completely silent about the years between this Temple visit and his baptism. Indirectly, we learn that he had several sisters and brothers, that he probably worked as a carpenter, that he was well liked, but attracted little or no special attention. He surely went to school, for he read Hebrew and spoke and understood Aramaic—and in all likelihood, Greek.

Jesus' public ministry began when he was baptized by his

cousin John. **(Read Mark 1:9-11.)** This baptism was an anointment, a recognition of special status and consecration for a special ministry. According to Matthew, John believed that Jesus was already so "special" that he needed no such baptism. Jesus, however, insisted on it, thereby firmly identifying himself with us in our human condition (see Matthew 3:13-17).

What was his special ministry to be? His decision about that began while being tempted by the devil. After that experience, "Jesus came to Galilee, proclaiming the good news of God, and saying, 'The time is fulfilled, and the kingdom of God has come near; repent, and believe in the good news'" (Mark 1:14-15). His mission, for now, was to preach, teach, and heal both physical and spiritual illness. He walked the dusty roads of Galilee from village to village, doing just that: meeting and associating with all kinds of people. The Cross would come later.

CLOSING PRAYER: Eternal God, our loving Father: We thank you for the Babe of Bethlehem and for the Christ he became. Perfect in obedience to you, he loved us so much that he suffered and died a painful human death for our salvation. Thank you, LORD. Amen.

Questions for Reflection or Discussion

1. Try to imagine all the experiences Jesus might have had as a newborn baby in a poor village family until, at age twelve, he discussed religion with the rabbis. How does that affect your thoughts about him?
2. Review Mark's account of Jesus' baptism (1:9-11). What does it show about his divinity? About his humanity?
3. Recall your baptism. [Recognition and consecration] What meaning and importance does that have for you today?
4. Do you feel that God has recognized you as his daughter or son? If so, how does that affect your daily living?

27
Food for Whose Children?

Matthew 15:21-28; Mark 7:24-30

OPENING PRAYER: We are thankful, our Father, that you love all of us and take care of our needs. You send sunshine and rain, cold and warmth which sustain all life. You provide us with beautiful flowers, and with vegetables as food for our bodies. Animals flourish to supply us with meat and milk for food, and pets keep us company. We are especially thankful, O God, for your love revealed in the Christ, who is the Savior of the world. He is the Savior of people of all ages, races, and places. He is the Light of life for us here, now. Therefore, we pray together as Jesus taught us, saying The Lord's Prayer . . . .

LESSON: We continue our study of Jesus as Savior of the whole world, with a text from the Gospel of Matthew. Mark also reports the same event in Jesus' life. Both proclaim the gospel of God's forgiving, saving love for all his children, including you and me.

Right after his baptism by John in the Jordan, Jesus was deciding exactly what it was that God wanted him to do. The devil got into the act by tempting him while he was out in the desert, hungry. He was offered three ways to use his special, divine powers. Jesus had to decide: Are they God's way? You remember them:

1. "Turn stones to bread": that is, use his power to feed the body, to devote himself to the physical and economic welfare of his people. There were lots of hungry people, but his answer was: "Man shall not live by bread alone, but by every word that proceedeth out of the mouth of God" (Matthew 4:4 KJV). We need physical food, but Jesus' call was first to preach the saving Word of God to hungry souls.

2. "Jump off the top of the Temple": that is, pull off a miracle to attract a mass of followers, who would be attracted for the wrong reasons—not because they recognized that he could bring them the bread of life, but because they wanted excitement, thrills.

3. "I'll give you all the kingdoms of the world": that is, be a powerful political and military leader—which was exactly the kind of Messiah most Jews expected. However, that was not God's way to save and care for people.

So Jesus came back from the desert and began to preach, teach, and heal—bodies *and* souls. That was his calling, but to whom was he called? Certainly to the Jews. Messiah, God's anointed one, was a Jewish hope and expectation.

Our text in Matthew reports what happened when Jesus left the country of the Jews and went into a foreign country. (**Read Matthew 15:21-29.**) This is a surprising, gripping story. To understand it fully we must remember at least two things. First, Jesus was seriously considering the question: To whom is God sending me? For whom is God's saving love given? Second, Jesus had a quick wit and a sense of humor. His mind was "sharp as a tack," and so was this woman's. Both of them used words cleverly and, in part, humorously, to make their points. Let us look at the story again, with these things in mind.

The woman is a noisy foreigner. She follows Jesus and his disciples, shouting for his help. His disciples, all Jews, have been trained to think of a Messiah as being for the Jews. If he helps this non-Jew, what will they think?

So he speaks, perhaps as a response to them, and perhaps partly as a question: "I was sent *only* to the children of Israel?" In any case, the woman disagrees.

She falls at his feet, saying over and over, "My child, my daughter needs your help, too!" Then begins their half joking but deadly serious conversation. To get the fine points of this passage of Scripture we must note that Matthew used a special Greek word for "dog," one meaning "little dog" or "puppy." Knowing what we do about Jesus, we do not believe he thought of this woman and her child as "dogs." Rather, Jesus was making a comparison between "little dogs" and "children." We might interpret their conversation this way:

Jesus: "You don't *really* take the children's food and throw it into the yard for the little dogs, do you?"

Woman: "You're right, Sir; but even the puppies under the table get the children's leftovers, don't they?"

Thus, this devoted, persistent mother, with quick wit and clever tongue, firmed up the decision of Jesus' heart, already yearning toward *all* God's children. He never turned back. On the Cross, he died for all. God is love. He loves *you*. He loves even me.

CLOSING PRAYER: Eternal God: You are our Father; we are all your children; rich or poor, sick or well, young or old, good or bad. You love and take care of each of us. We are thankful. Alleluia! Amen.

Questions for Reflection or Discussion

1. Most Christians take for granted that Jesus is Savior of the whole world. Does it help you appreciate his sacrificial life and death to think that he had to *choose* to be God's Messiah? Why? Or why not?
2. Matthew, Mark, and Luke all report Jesus' temptations in the desert. Can you see how each temptation tested both his human nature and his divine calling? How is that related to your understanding of the doctrine of the Incarnation—God with us in human form?
3. Does today's text help you to see Jesus as being human, like we are? How do you make important decisions in your life?
4. What does Jesus' conversation with the foreign woman tell you about him? About her?

28
God Is Love

Mark 1:40-42, 10:32-34; Matthew 26:37-39;
Luke 9:51, 22:44, 23:34; John 8:2-11; Romans 5:8b

OPENING PRAYER: Eternal and loving God: Help us to know you better, so that we can return your love more faithfully. We are thankful that you have revealed yourself so that we *can* know you and have a personal relationship with you. We see your wisdom and power revealed in the world you created. Scripture tells us of your actions in the history of the children of Israel, your people of the Old Covenant. We are especially thankful for the forgiving love revealed in your Son Jesus, the Lord of our New Covenant. Now we pray together, using the words he taught us, saying The Lord's Prayer . . . .

LESSON: What is God like? What is his nature and the nature of our relationship with him? In a way, the whole Bible answers that question: "God is love" (1 John 4:8). Again and again, Scripture reveals that God is loving and kind; that he loves us, his children; that he is concerned about us and our welfare. We see this most clearly in the life and death of Jesus.

This lesson begins a series summarizing the nature of God as revealed in Jesus' actions, teachings, and death. Of course, God's power, wisdom, love, and glory are much too great for us to grasp and understand completely. However, Scripture reveals enough for us to live by, and to die with. The following Scriptures reveal the extent of Divine Love when incarnate in the human flesh of Jesus.

97

Mark reports that early in his ministry, Jesus was walking the roads of Galilee when a leper came to him. (**Read Mark 1:40-42.**) Lepers were considered loathsome. People would not get close to, much less touch, one. Jesus had the power to heal the man from a "safe distance." But Jesus, who was God's love in human form, was "moved with pity." He reached out his hand and *touched* him. The love of God was thus revealed as personal, intimate, compassionate.

(**Read John 8:2-11.**) The woman was caught in the very act of adultery; she was brought to Jesus to be judged. The Law of Moses said she should be stoned to death. Jesus forgave her, showing that God loves, accepts, and forgives even the worst sinners.

The ultimate revelation that God is love was made by Jesus' sacrificial death. As Paul wrote, "While we still were sinners, Christ died for us" (Romans 5:8).

Several passages of Scripture about Jesus' last days on earth help us deeply appreciate the love of God in Christ. One tells of his last trip from Galilee to Jerusalem to celebrate Passover. He knew the Cross was waiting on Golgotha, but he went anyway. While on the road, Jesus told the Twelve what was coming. (**Read Mark 10:32-34.**) The disciples did not understand. Jesus knew what was ahead and, as Luke reports, "He steadfastly set his face to go to Jerusalem" (Luke 9:51 TAB).

After his Last Supper, Jesus went into the privacy of the Garden of Gethsemane to pray. (**Read Matthew 26:37-39.**) Three times he uttered his anguished prayer, while "his sweat became like great drops of blood falling down on the ground" (Luke 22:44).

The God of Love agonizes for our well-being. He is determined to save us for abundant, eternal life with him. Luke reports this word from the Cross. Jesus, divinity in human form, loved the Roman soldiers who had driven nails through his hands and feet, and he prayed: "Father, forgive them; for they do not know what they are doing" (Luke 23:34).

What is God like? There can be no doubt: God is love. He loves all his children. He loves you and me, now and forever. That is indeed Good News! Thanks be to God!

CLOSING PRAYER: Dear God: You are our loving parent. You love and take care of us. You are determined to save us for abundant, eternal life in heaven with you. Thank you, LORD. Amen.

Questions for Reflection or Discussion

1. What do you, personally, conclude from the fact that Jesus cured a loathsome leper by actually touching him, and forgave a woman who had broken one of the Ten Commandments? Does God really love, forgive, and heal everyone?
2. If God the Father, instead of Jesus, had been judging the woman taken in adultery, would he have said, "Neither do I condemn thee, go and sin no more?" Why or why not?
3. Jesus' agonized prayer in the Garden and his death on the Cross are the ultimate proof that "Christian love" is self-sacrificing love for others. It can be genuine without requiring death. Have you ever seen anyone you know approximate this ideal? Describe his or her behavior.
4. What self-sacrificing actions of love have you done for others, because you're a Christian?

29

God Forgives
Even the Worst Sinner

John 8:2-11

OPENING PRAYER: O God, our Heavenly Father: You give us many gifts for which we are thankful: life, food, family, and friends who are interested in us and help us take care of our daily needs. We are especially thankful, LORD, for your love revealed in Jesus Christ our Savior. It is a forgiving love, a saving love that covers all your children—right here where we are and everywhere in the world. This love is the Good News, the Gospel Truth, revealed in the life, teachings, death, and resurrection of your Son Jesus Christ, our Lord. Therefore, let us pray together, using the words he taught us, saying The Lord's Prayer . . . .

LESSON: We continue our study of the loving nature of God. We've seen how the God of love is revealed in the Old Testament —in the prophet Hosea, in the Prophet of the Exile, and in Lamentations. Now we find the same message in the events of Jesus' life.

The basic Good News of the Bible may be stated thus: God created us in love. He sustains us by his love. He forgives us *because* he loves us—no matter who we are. When we die, he folds us into his everlasting, loving arms. As beautiful and comforting as this sounds, sometimes we have trouble believing it. Does God *really* forgive *everyone?* Will he really forgive *any* sin? Jesus answers, "Yes!"

The commandment "You shall not commit adultery" (Exodus 20:14) was especially important for Jews, in Old Testament times and in Jesus' day. Then it was considered much worse for a woman to commit adultery than it was for a man; it was unforgivable. Jesus demonstrated that if God forgives that sin, he will forgive anything. He does and he will, "for the Bible tells me so."

(Read John 8:2-11.) The Jewish law clearly stated that such a woman be stoned to death (the man too, but where was he?). Here were a bunch of men wanting to kill the woman and also hoping to test Jesus. Jesus preached a message of forgiving love, but their law called for capital punishment. The religious leaders thought they had Jesus in a trap. If he kept on preaching this gospel of love, he would undermine the law. If he forgave this sinful woman, he would defy the law, and they could arrest him. They were putting Jesus to a hard test. Which is more important: the law or God's love?

Jesus was in a tight spot. What was he thinking, as he wrote in the dust at his feet? Could the Pharisees see it? What *did* he write? Finally, he straightened up, looked them in the eye, and said, "OK, go ahead and kill her. But, the first rock must be thrown by one of you who has *never* sinned." Stunned silence. The Bible says, "They all left, one by one, the older ones first" (v. 9 GNB). Could they look him in the eye?

Why did the older ones leave first? Were they the most guilty, having had more time to sin? Or were they mature enough to have at least a glimpse of God's love? Finally, everyone was gone; only Jesus was there with the woman standing before him, waiting for his judgment. Jesus, God in human form, gave it: "Neither do I condemn thee. Go and sin no more" (v. 11 KJV).

Yes, there is forgiveness for any sin—forgiveness that sets you free to live a new life, trusting God and his love. It is forgiveness that gives you freedom from guilt, freedom for new life in Christ, and help from the Holy Spirit to go and sin no more. Yes, the love of God does forgive anyone, for anything. His love for each of his children, for each one of us, is so great that he is ready to forgive us anything, when we repent. But as we explored in a previous lesson, repentance is more than saying, "I'm sorry; please forgive me." It requires a change in behavior, a decision to turn around and walk in a different direction, to walk with God, to live the "new life in Christ"—with God's Holy Spirit helping us. Whatever your sin, or mine, God's love and forgiveness are waiting for us when we come home to him.

CLOSING PRAYER: Father, our loving divine parent: We are thankful for the depth and breadth and strength of your steadfast love for everyone, even for me. Thank you, LORD. Amen.

Questions for Reflection or Discussion

1. Have you ever thought that some act or thought of yours was truly unforgivable, and you doubted that God could forgive you? If so, what did you do? What happened? If you still feel unforgiven, carefully read Ephesians 2:4-12; Romans 3:23-24, 5:6-12; and Galatians 2:1*a*, 3:23-28 (see lesson 34) to find the Bible's Good News of God's love and grace for you.
2. What do you consider the worst sin? Will God forgive this sin? Why or why not?
3. What do the words "repent" and "repentance" mean to you personally? Describe an instance when you think someone truly repented? Describe another when someone *seemed* to be penitent, but really was not? What was lacking?
4. What is a person's life like after true repentance? What is one freed *from?* Freed *for?* What help is available to a person trying to "go, and sin no more"? Be specific, illustrating from your own life or that of someone you know well.

30
God Searches for Us, and Waits

Luke 15:1-32

OPENING PRAYER: Eternal creating God, father of our Lord Jesus Christ: We are thankful that the words of Scripture are Good News. They tell us that "God is Love," that you "so loved the world" that your Divinity came to earth in Jesus to save everyone—even me. We are thankful that you love us, that you forgive and save the good and bad, old and young, those who are cheerful and the grouchy ones with long faces. All of us are your children. That is indeed Good News. Be with us in this time of Bible study. Help us to hear clearly and know deeply the Word you have for us today. And now we pray together, using the words Jesus taught us, saying The Lord's Prayer . . . .

LESSON: All the lessons in this book announce one truth: God is love. That is the main message of Scripture; the *whole* Bible should be read in relation to that central fact about God, the God and Father of our Lord Jesus Christ. The God of the Old Testament is the same God of forgiving love who revealed himself in Jesus in the New Testament. As we read in Psalm 145, "The LORD is gracious and merciful, slow to anger and abounding in steadfast love" (v. 8). Three of Jesus' parables illustrate this well.

(**Read Luke 15:1-7.**) We all know about that lost sheep. While he or she has run away, the ninety-nine good, faithful sheep are obediently browsing or sleeping in some green pasture. The Good Shepherd leaves them and goes off searching for the one bad one. He does not just sit and wait for it to come back. No, he goes out looking, high and low; over the hills and into the valleys. How long does he look? A couple of hours? Until it gets dark? No. Jesus said he looks "until he finds it." That might take days. For some of us, it takes years! But God loves each of us, so he keeps on looking and looking.

When the lost one is found, the shepherd carries it home and calls in friends and neighbors for a happy celebration.

Jesus said, "I tell you, there will be more joy in heaven over one sinner who repents than over ninety-nine righteous persons who need no repentance" (v. 7). Are there really some folks who never need to repent? Or, was Paul right when he wrote that "all have sinned" (Romans 3:23)?

(Read Luke 15:8-10.) Here Jesus used a woman to illustrate what God is like. This time nothing is said about the "righteous," except that the owner knows where they are, safe in their usual box or hiding place. Otherwise, the two stories give the same message. The owner looks, and looks diligently—not for some reasonable time, but until the lost one is found. Again there is celebration, not for all those safe in the box, but for the one being returned. Even the angels in heaven, Jesus said, rejoice over each sinner who returns.

The third parable (Luke 15:11-32) is so familiar we do not need to read it. (You may choose to do so.) We call it "The Prodigal Son." More accurately, it is "The Loving Father" who has two sons. The young one wants his half of the inheritance so that he can leave the dull old farm and live it up in the city. He does just that, while his brother stays home and works hard every day. In a far country, the prodigal son blows all his money on wine, women, and song. He really hits bottom in a pigpen, so hungry that he envies the well-fed pigs. The shock treatment wakes him up. So he plans and carefully rehearses a speech, asking his father's forgiveness and begging to be taken back as a hired servant.

In this parable the father does not go out searching. I imagine him standing on the front porch every evening after work, looking down the road, waiting, hoping the lost one will return. One evening he does see him way down the road—walking mighty slow, practicing his repentance speech. The father doesn't wait for him to get home. The father has *already* forgiven him. He runs down the road and, before the son can say a word, he hugs him, kisses him, gives him new clothes, and promises him a big party to celebrate his homecoming. The father says, "For this son of mine was dead, and now he is alive; he was lost, but now he has been found" (v. 24 GNB).

Jesus' teaching is clear: God has a special interest in and concern for the sinner. He or she is not cast out or blown away like chaff, but is sought out and brought back home to a joyful welcome. Remember the words of this old hymn: "Earnestly, tenderly, Jesus is calling, calling, O sinner, come home!" That's the gospel, the Good News. I like to hear that good news; I *need* to hear it.

But what about the ninety-nine sheep safe at home, the coins safe in the box, the brother who stayed home and worked hard? What kind of news does the New Testament have for them? Jesus never suggests that God does not love the "good folks." It is just that he is deeply concerned for the lost, and full of joy over one new soul who returns to him. When the faithful older brother complains about the celebration for his returned brother and refuses to come in to the party, the father goes out looking for him, too, and invites him in. "But you never gave a party for *me!*" the older son complains. Jesus said that the father replies, "Son, you are always with me, and all that is mine is yours" (v. 31). The New Testament message, the message of Jesus, is that *everyone* (the good, the bad, and the in-between) is a child of the same loving Father. That's the Gospel Truth.

CLOSING PRAYER: Heavenly Father: Jesus, by his words and by his deeds, shows us that your nature is infinite love. You love, cherish, and forgive all your children. Your loving and forgiving heart has a special concern for those we call sinners. You go looking for them. You wait for them to come home, and you celebrate their return joyfully. That is Good News to our ears and to our hearts. Thank you, LORD. Amen.

Questions for Reflection or Discussion

1. Do the Old and New Testaments agree that the LORD is a God of forgiving love? Whether your answer is "yes" or "no," what makes you think so?

2. Jesus emphasized God's special concern for the lost sheep, the lost coin, the lost or wandering person. How does that make you think about God, about yourself, and about your relationship with God?

3. Jesus used three human beings to illustrate God's love for the lost: a shepherd, the father of two sons, and a house-wife. Is God like a woman? Is a woman like God, in some ways? Does Genesis 1:27 help answer those questions?

4. *Home* is a key idea in these parables. God *searches* for the lost and celebrates when they are safe back home. Some-times God *waits* for the wanderer to come home, then celebrates. When the faithful brother sulks outside the house, the father goes out to plead with him to "come in." What goes through your own mind and heart, when you think of the God of love searching and waiting, and of his invitations to "come home"?

31
God Loves Both Sinners
and the Righteous

Luke 15:11-32

OPENING PRAYER: Loving Heavenly Father: We thank you for so many things. We thank you for life: even with all its ups and downs, pains and joys. Life is your gift to us. We thank you for family and friends. Throughout life, we have known friendship and love. We thank you for food and shelter, and for neighbors, with whom we share our experiences, our problems, our memories, and our hopes. For all these we are thankful. Most of all, Father, we are grateful for your steadfast and eternal love, revealed in the life and teachings of Jesus Christ, your Son, our Lord. Using the words he taught us, we now pray together, saying The Lord's Prayer . . . .

LESSON: We continue to study God's forgiving love as revealed in the life and teachings of Jesus. We know that God loves, forgives, and wants to save everybody, yet we still have questions about God's love. Surely God is more interested in the righteous. Doesn't he love us good church folks more than obvious sinners? There are some passages in the Old Testament that may lead us to believe that. Psalm 1, for instance, says that "the LORD watches over the way of the righteous, but the way of the wicked will perish" (v. 6). Note, however, it does not say that the wicked *people* will perish; rather, their *way of life* will perish. God tries to call sinners from wickedness to a better way. In Jesus' parables about a lost sheep, a lost coin, and a prodigal son, which we studied in the last lesson, Jesus makes it perfectly clear that our forgiving God seeks out his wayward children.

Does that mean, then, that God loves the sinners more than the righteous? Not at all; and that is what this lesson is about.

Let us take a fresh look at the *whole* parable of the loving father who has two sons and loves them both, equally, but in different ways.

(Read Luke 15:11-32.) Jesus told this story to illustrate the nature of God and his relationship with us. The story parallels our human experience. Imagine that a father and mother have two boys. One does his homework and makes good grades in school. He works weekends and pays part of his room and board. The other one has dropped out of school, hangs around on street corners, stays out till all hours, and finally runs away to the city. Which son do the parents spend more time thinking about? Which are they more concerned about? The prodigal, right? And when the prodigal finally comes home, it is a time to celebrate.

In the parable, the father throws a big party. How does big brother react? Is he happy to see his brother? No way! He reacts in a very human way. Does it look like an unloving reaction? It is. He does not act like one created in the image of his loving father. He acts like a self-righteous, normal human being. It's evening. He is coming home from the fields, where he has worked hard all day. He sees lights and hears the music. What's going on? He finds that his father is celebrating his brother's return home. He is so mad that he sulks outdoors and won't come into the house. And father? Just as with the other son, he hurried to this one, too.

But the elder son talks back to him: "What have you ever done for me? I've worked faithfully and you've never given me even a goat to barbecue with my friends! But you gave this, this 'delinquent' son of yours [not 'my brother'] a new suit of clothes, a prime-rib dinner, and a party with a dance band!"

Can you hear the patient, tender love in the father's voice?: "Son, you are always with me, and all that is mine is yours" (v. 31). "I love you, too. Come on into my house, it is your home." As Psalm 1 says: "The LORD knows the way of the righteous" (v. 6 RSV). He has known and been close to this son all the time.

The last part of the parable contains two important messages. First, God loves both the sinners and the righteous, even when they are "self-righteous." He loves them equally; but, like human parents, he loves them in different ways because they are different. Both are welcome in his eternal home, *when* they come in.

Second, we are warned that there are risks in being "good and faithful servants," respectable churchgoing folks. It is easy to feel that we've "got it made," that we are better than God's wayward children. It is easy to look down on, or avoid, them. We may resent the special attention, the extra time and concern that God's love—and sometimes the Church—gives to the wandering ones. But God loves us anyway. He just has to spend more time persuading some of us to come home—and stay there.

CLOSING PRAYER: Merciful God: the Bible tells of your fatherly love, of your forgiving, saving love for all your daughters and sons, in all times and all places, even for us today. This Gospel Truth is revealed in the life and teachings of Jesus, especially his death on the Cross. For that amazing grace we say: "Thank you, LORD." Amen.

Questions for Reflection or Discussion

1. What do you understand the Bible to mean when it says that "the *way* of the wicked will perish"? When will that "way" perish? Now?

2. In the parable of the father with two sons, do you see yourself as one of the sons, or as some mixture of both? If the younger, what message comes to you from Jesus? How does that make you feel? What does it suggest that you say or do? If the elder, what is the message for you? How does that make you feel? What does it suggest that you say or do?

3. Have you known human parents with one responsible and one prodigal child? How did they feel about, act toward, "love" each one? Has this happened in your family?

4. Can we really believe that God invites and welcomes all persons into his Kingdom? What do we do to receive his gift?

32
God Says:
Latecomers Are Welcome

Matthew 20:1-15

OPENING PRAYER: O God, Father of our Lord Jesus Christ: We are thankful that you are our Father, too. You love and watch over us, your children. You hold out your arms to each of us, inviting us to join you in your heavenly kingdom. Its gates are open. You even come searching for us. We are thankful for this Good News in Scripture. Help us to hear it today and accept it into our hearts. Help us to live, and to die, trusting in your love and grace. Jesus taught this message, and we pray together, using the words he gave us, saying The Lord's Prayer . . . .

LESSON: We continue to study what Jesus revealed about the Grace of God, the unearned and undeserved gift of forgiving love, which he has for every one of his children. Saint Paul called it "salvation by grace through faith." We are saved when we believe and trust in God's unfailing, steadfast love.

In previous lessons, we have discovered how God welcomes each of us when we come home. But how long will God wait for *me* to "come home," to sign up in his Kingdom and receive the full rewards of his love? What if I don't show up until the last minute? Jesus answered these questions with a parable that shows that even latecomers are welcomed into the Kingdom of God, on the same basis as everyone else.

(Read Matthew 20:1-15.) God, like the owner of the vineyard, is out recruiting all day. The owner was looking for people to join his team. He went out on the streets, into the marketplace. He invited everyone he saw. Surprise! Whether they came to work at 7:00 A.M. or 5:00 P.M., they all got exactly the same pay. Why? The Bible gives two reasons:

First, God is generous; that is, his heart overflows with love enough to go around to everyone. Second, God is in control; he can do what he chooses with what is his—his resources, his love, anything.

It pleases God to treat all alike. He chooses to accept and receive everybody—early or late, old or young, rich or poor, women or men, "good" or "bad"—everyone who comes to him, who signs on as a member of his team. All of us are equal in God's eyes, and he loves each of us equally—yet differently, because we are different from one another. All are welcome, even when we arrive very late. That is the Gospel Truth, the Good News of God's Grace.

CLOSING PRAYER: O God: we are thankful that you are our Father; that we are your children. You love each of us, always. You love us enough to invite us into your eternal Kingdom of Love, to live with you in that mansion with enough rooms for all of us. Your gracious forgiving love makes it easy for us to live, and to die, trusting in you. Thank you, LORD. Amen.

Questions for Reflection or Discussion

1. Do you know some mature person who has never joined the Church and says, "It's too late; what good would it do now?" How have you answered his or her question? After lessons 28–32, do you have anything different to say? What?
2. Read Matthew 20:13-15, preferably in the words of several translations. Can you put into your own words the reasons God rewards everyone equally? What are they?
3. Because everyone ("good" or "bad," early or late) shares God's love equally, how should the earlybirds and the latecomers think about and treat one another? Should it be the same within a church as it generally is in the community?
4. Do you feel any jealousy toward the latecomers whom God loves? How would you answer someone who says they're waiting until the very end of their life to become a Christian? What are they missing by waiting so long?

33
Love:
Divine and Human

Luke 7:36-47; John 13:34; 1 John 4:16, 19

OPENING PRAYER: Heavenly Father: We thank you for this new day, and for the opportunity to come together again in your Name to seek your Word in Scripture. We are especially thankful, LORD, for your steadfast forgiving love, revealed in your Son, Jesus Christ, our Lord and Savior. We are grateful that he loved us enough to suffer and die for our salvation. We pray together, using the words he taught us, saying The Lord's Prayer . . . .

LESSON: Most everyone has a favorite Bible verse. For many, it is "God is love" (1 John 4:16), because it sums up the central message of Scripture. As we've seen in previous lessons, both Old and New Testaments tell over and over, in many ways, the Good News of God's steadfast, forgiving love for all his children. Part of the Bible's Good News about love is that even imperfect human beings are capable of loving and forgiving. God created us in his own image, "Male and female created he them" (Genesis 1:27). We are certainly not gods; not even angels! However, since God is love and we are created in his image, we have some capacity for loving. Jesus knew that.

He said to his followers, "I give you a new commandment, that you love one another. Just as I have loved you, you also should love one another" (John 13:34). The Bible shows us human, as well as Divine love. Remember Ruth's love for her mother-in-law (lesson 6) and Hosea's love for his unfaithful wife (lesson 16).

This lesson attempts to answer the question: What makes it possible for us to love unselfishly and to forgive? As noted, we are created in God's image and have the capacity to love and forgive. However, how do we *call out and use* our capacity to love? First, we have Jesus as a model to follow; and we have the Holy Spirit to guide us. Second, our loving springs from our having been loved. Our power to love is released by our experience of being loved—by mother, father, brothers, sisters, and friends; but most of all by the love of God, the Father, Son, and the Holy Spirit. "We love, because he first loved us" (1 John 4:19).

Today's Scripture from the Gospel of Luke reports an event that illustrates how the experience of forgiving love releases our capacity for loving. You know the story about the woman who washed Jesus' feet with her tears and dried them with her hair. Some facts may help you understand the message communicated by this event. Jesus was invited to dinner by a Pharisee, a rather self-satisfied religious leader. It was customary to greet guests, especially honored ones, by providing water to wash their dusty feet, dressing their hair with oil, and greeting them with a kiss on each cheek. They did not sit in chairs around a tall table as we do. Their table was low, and they reclined on couches. (**Read Luke 7:36-47.**)

You and I have received a wealth of God's forgiving love. When we experience forgiveness and deeply feel how much we have been loved, especially by God the Father and his Son Jesus Christ, then we are freed and enabled to love and forgive our fellow human beings. Then we can follow Jesus' commandment to "love one another."

CLOSING PRAYER: Eternal God, our Father: We thank you for your love, especially as it is revealed in Jesus Christ our Lord and Savior. We thank you for your forgiveness. We pray that now you will send your Holy Spirit to guide us and empower us, so that we too *can* and *will* love and forgive others. For Jesus' sake. Amen.

Questions for Reflection or Discussion

1. Do you find it a joy or a burden to have a God-given capacity to love and forgive? Why?

2. Describe an experience of yours, or of someone you know well, in which acts of love and forgiveness beget other acts of love and forgiveness? How was the relationship between giver and receiver affected?
3. If you had been at the dinner when the woman crashed the party as she did, what would you have thought about her? About what Jesus said? Looking back from your present perspective, would you react differently? In what way?
4. Are there people in our society who are hard for you to love? What has been the most difficult experience in your life in which you followed Jesus' commandment to *love one another?*

34
Saint Paul:
Salvation by Grace

Ephesians 2:5-10; Romans 3:23-24; 5:6-10; Galatians 2:16; 3:23-28

OPENING PRAYER: Our Heavenly Father: We are thankful that you have brought us together again in Jesus' name to study your Word in Scripture. Send your Holy Spirit to guide our minds and hearts, so that each of us may hear what you are trying to tell us. Help us to understand how much you love and care for each person. Help us to hear and cherish the Good News of your forgiving love. Help us to understand more clearly what you did for us in the life, death, and resurrection of Jesus, the Christ, our Lord. And now we pray together, using the words he taught us, saying The Lord's Prayer . . . .

LESSON: The previous six lessons have presented examples of the truth that God is love. This lesson is a summary, based on Saint Paul's writings on the Gospel, an old English word which some scholars believe means both "good news," or "glad tidings," and "God Speak"—what God says. It is the Good News of God's forgiving love for each one of his many children. It is the gift God gave us through Jesus, his Son and our Savior.

The joy of the gospel filled Jesus' disciples after his resurrection and the visitation of the Holy Spirit at Pentecost. They went out from Jerusalem in every direction, preaching the gospel throughout the world, until it came to us. Paul, the last of the apostles, traveled most, went farthest, and preached to more people in more places than any other apostle. So it is fitting that we conclude this section by studying letters he wrote to early Christian churches, in which we find the best description of the Good News, the Gospel of Jesus Christ. From Paul, we get the subtitle of this lesson, "Salvation by Grace."

Paul's statements tend to be rather abstract and theological in contrast to the concrete, everyday, personal examples we have in Jesus' own behavior and parables. However, what Paul wrote to early Christians summarized for them the Good News he had found in Jesus. It can do the same for us.

In essence, Paul says: We are not saved by being good, not even by *trying* to be good. We do not have to deserve God's love. We need not earn his love. We cannot. He made us and has loved us always. God knows that we are human beings, not angels. He knows that we are sinners. We cannot make ourselves perfect. God loves us in spite of our imperfections, our sins, our failures. He loved us enough to become human flesh in Jesus of Nazareth. As Jesus, he loved us enough to suffer, bleed, and die on the Cross for our salvation.

What do we have to do? Only believe—that is, have faith. Trust in God's forgiving love, revealed in Christ Jesus. All we need do is accept the fact that God accepts us, just as we are. It is God's love for us that enables us to love others and to do good deeds.

No one preached this Good News better than Paul, who wrote, "By grace you have been saved through faith" (Ephesians 2:8). "Grace" is one of the sweetest words in the Bible. Grace is the freely given, the unearned and undeserved love of God, revealed in Christ.

"Everyone has sinned and is far away from God's saving presence. But by the free gift of God's grace all are put right with him through Christ Jesus, who sets them free" (Romans 3:23-24 GNB). Grace sets us free: free from God's anger; free for a new life in Christ; free to love and serve God by loving and serving others.

Let us explore several passages from Paul's letters to early Christian congregations in Rome, Galatia, and Ephesus. (**Read Romans 5:6-10.**) We know, and God knows, that "everyone has sinned" (Romans 3:23 GNB). The Good News is that we are forgiven sinners; not that we *can* be forgiven, but we *already have been* forgiven. It happened when Jesus suffered and died on the Cross for each and every human being who ever lived, or will live.

We all know the beautiful verse that begins, "God so loved the world that he gave his only Son" (John 3:16). Paul said that to die for an enemy is contrary to human nature. We find it next to impossible to die even for a friend. Divine love goes far, far beyond that. Jesus died on the cross, painfully, for sinners, for us.

Paul experienced the Jewish Law as a set of rules and regulations about what people should and should not do. He wrote, "We know that a person is put right with God only through faith in Jesus Christ, never by doing what the Law requires" (Galatians 2:16 GNB). Before meeting Jesus, Paul had thought that you won favor with God by following those rules. As a Pharisee, he had tried hard to keep the Law. He found it an impossible burden.

In Jesus, he found freedom from the burden of sin and shared it with people everywhere. By "faith in Christ," Paul did not mean "belief," as much as "trust"—trust in Jesus and in God's love. In place of a long list of do's and don'ts, we Christians are given a few basic principles to live by, such as love and justice. We are given a life guided and motivated by God's love, as revealed and illustrated in the life and teachings of Jesus. When our lives are focused on Christ, when he is the model for our behavior, we are guided in our decisions about what to do and what not to do.

(Read Galatians 3:23-28.) The Good News of God's forgiving love is for everyone, without exception or distinction. Paul saw that inequalities such as race, economic class, and gender were erased. All people are equally valued by God, all are forgiven and saved by God's freely given, undeserved Grace.

(Read Ephesians 2:4-10.) Here, Paul repeats that we do not need to earn God's forgiving love with so-called "good deeds," or any other way. God has made us, and he loves us. He does not save us because we are "good." What goodness we have is God's gift. We are able to do good things *because* he saved us. When we realize how much God loves us, when we accept the fact that he accepts us—then we are saved.

To that, Paul adds an important new fact about the grace of God: We are saved *from* guilt and fear; we are saved *for* life with Christ, a new life in which we have been "created for good works." When, through the Grace of God, Christ lives in us and we in him, *then* we can do good deeds. That is Good News.

CLOSING PRAYER: O God, our loving Father: You are revealed to us in Jesus' suffering love for all. We are thankful that you made us, that you accept us, and that you love and take care of us, no matter who or what we are. When we believe this, when we live trusting in your love, then we are saved. Thank you, LORD, for your amazing grace. Amen.

Questions for Reflection or Discussion

1. Think of a specific time when you felt unworthy of God's love. What did you think, feel, and do? Describe a time, place, and way in which you received reassurance of God's forgiving love.
2. Have you ever tried to earn God's love? Did you succeed? Why or why not?
3. Have you received some gift of God's grace recently? If so, how were your thoughts, feelings, and general behavior affected?
4. Think of a time when you forgave someone. How did you feel about yourself? About the other person? About God?
5. Does this lesson about God's grace remind you of any favorite hymns? Sing them, or say their words out loud. How do these hymns help you in daily living?

35
The Lord's Prayer

Matthew 6:9-13; Luke 11:2-4

OPENING PRAYER: O God our Father: We come to you again in prayer. Often we do not know how to pray as we should. However, when words fail, the Holy Spirit intercedes for us when we can only sigh or even groan. We stand in need of your guidance and especially your forgiveness. We want your help in facing the trials and temptations in our lives. O LORD, give us understanding minds and trusting hearts so that we may truly pray the prayer Jesus taught us, saying together The Lord's Prayer . . . .

LESSON: The aim of this lesson, and the next two, is to understand prayer better, to pray more deeply, to make prayer a more important part of our lives. We begin with the Lord's Prayer. This model that Jesus gave his disciples is recorded in both Matthew and Luke, in somewhat different words. We have said the words so many times that they may have lost their meaning for us. They are important words, however: Jesus gave them to guide *all* our praying.

No one can tell you how to pray. Each of us must pray out of our own trust in God, and within our own relationship with him. The following facts and ideas, however, may help you form your own understanding of this familiar prayer and of prayer in general. The Lord's Prayer begins:

Our Father. Prayer begins when God comes first, when, as it were, we "stand at attention" before God. True prayer occurs when we recognize that God is not "mine" but "ours." He is the God of all races, classes, and nations. When we pray this prayer, we pray not just for ourselves, but for and with all God's children.

119

Jesus called God "Father." We pray to one who is our parent; one who gave us life; one who loves, protects, and instructs us as his children. All of us are sisters and brothers.

In Heaven. God is high and lifted up, over all and above all. In his presence, we are in awe, reverent—lost in wonder. Heaven is a divine Kingdom where God's name is holy, where his rule is complete, and where his will is done obediently. God's rules of love and justice are fully practiced. The result is a community of shalom where there is peace without hostility or conflict, and security without anxiety or fear.

Holy be thy name; thy kingdom come, thy will be done on earth as it is in heaven. As children of God, we inherit citizenship in the heavenly community of Shalom. Jesus said, "The kingdom of heaven has come near" (Matthew 4:17). Therefore, we urgently desire, and pray, that life on this earth have the same conditions that make Heaven heavenly. That is, may God's name be so hallowed that it is the Name above all names. May God's reign and rule, his Kingdom, be as complete here on earth as it is in heaven. May his will be done here and now as obediently as it is in heaven. We ask God in his wisdom and power to make all this happen. We also should pray: "Father, help us, help *me,* to live like this: to put you first, to accept your rule over my life, to do your will obediently." If we live this way, the Kingdom is here, now, and we are members of it.

Give us this day our daily bread. The word "bread" stands for all our basic needs; but not everything we *want.* God gives us what his wisdom knows we really need. We pray that God will meet our needs for today only. Jesus said, "Do not be anxious about tomorrow" (Matthew 6:34 RSV). Each day is sufficient to itself. Manna in the desert fell one day's supply at a time. The future is in God's hands. The Greek words translated "daily bread" also can mean "bread for tomorrow" or "give us our bread day by day." Despite that humble, day-to-day perspective, it is perfectly all right to tell God what we want.

Forgive us our trespasses as we forgive those who trespass against us. This verse is the heart of the prayer, and of our relationship with God. Before we truly can pray for forgiveness, there are three questions we must answer, each in our own way.

First, exactly what is it we are asking to be forgiven? Luke and Matthew, in reporting this prayer, use different words for the idea they received from Jesus.

Matthew wrote, "Forgive us our debts, as we also have forgiven our debtors" (6:12). Then in verse 14, he talks about "trespasses." To us, "debts" and "trespasses" refer to economic matters: unpaid bills and entering someone else's property. Here they are symbols of something spiritual: sins. We sin when we do not discharge our obligations to God, when we do not repay him for what he has given us. His gift of love to us should be repaid with deep gratitude and loving service to others.

An even greater sin, perhaps, is "trespassing" on God's domain, acting as if we are God. We sin when we think and act as if we can do what only God can do. We sin when we do not trust God to run his world. Rather than trust our lives to him, we try to control our own lives and those of others.

Luke uses the word *sins:* "Forgive us our sins, for we ourselves forgive everyone indebted to us" (11:4). Many Christians today think we need to return to that good old-fashioned word *sin*. Perhaps it is only when we deeply feel and can say, "I am a sinner" that we can ask for God's forgiveness and really experience it.

Second, Jesus said "forgive us our sins"; why not "our Sin"? Because our basic, "original" sin was forgiven by the death of Jesus Christ on the Cross. There he atoned for our sin. We are sinners; but since the Cross, we are *forgiven* sinners. Even so, we still commit sins by doing things we should not do and not doing things we should, and we need to ask for forgiveness.

A third question is raised by the end of the sentence: God forgives us, *as we forgive others*. After the prayer ends with verse 13, Matthew adds these troubling words: "For if you forgive others their trespasses, your heavenly Father will also forgive you; but if you do not forgive others, neither will your Father forgive your trespasses" (6:14). Scholars think this is a comment added by Matthew, and were not the words of Jesus. They are not in Luke's report of the prayer.

Scholars suggest that Matthew added "For if you forgive others their trespasses, your heavenly Father will also forgive you," following the tradition reported in Mark's Gospel: "Whenever you stand praying, forgive, if you have anything against anyone; so that your Father in heaven may also forgive you your trespasses" (11:25). They suggest that he was very concerned that God's will actually be done in the Christian community, where the spirit of brotherhood was endangered.

When we ask God to "forgive us our sins as we are forgiving toward others," we are asking for God's help to forgive others, even our enemies, in response to God's forgiving love, freely given to us.

Lead us not into temptation, but deliver us from evil. God *allowed* Jesus to be tempted, but the devil was the tempter. Just as God allowed Jesus to be tempted, so God allows many everyday situations in which we can be tempted. Therefore, we need to be aware of God's presence with us in every life situation. We pray that God will not let us find temptation; but if we do, that he will help us make the right choice. We pray that he will deliver us, will save us from the power of evil at work in the world and, at times, in our own lives.

That is the prayer given us from the Lord Jesus, through Matthew and Luke. To it, the early Church added a declaration of praise and glory for the God to whom we pray: *For thine is the kingdom, and the power, and the glory for ever and ever.*

CLOSING PRAYER: Heavenly Father: Help us to pray with understanding minds and trusting hearts the words our Lord and Savior Jesus Christ taught us, saying together The Lord's Prayer . . . .

Questions for Reflection or Discussion

1. When you say the Lord's Prayer privately, in small groups, and in public worship, do you really *pray* it? If "yes," how can you tell? If "no," how might it become real prayer for you?
2. What, specifically, are you asking for when you ask God for "daily bread"? How do you feel, and what do you do when

you receive what you ask for? How do you feel and what do you do when you do not get what you ask for?

3. When you pray "forgive my trespasses (debts, sins) as I am forgiving toward others," do you *experience* God's forgiving love? What is that like? Does it help you to forgive others for the hurts that have made you resentful or bitter?

4. Do you believe that God loves us enough to forgive us, even if we have not forgiven every person who ever did us wrong? Why?

5. What temptations have you experienced? Did your faith help you to make the right choices? If yes, how? If not, how might you prepare for "next time"?

36
"Lord, Teach Us to Pray"

*Matthew 6:5-8; 26:39; Mark 1:35; Luke 5:15-16; 11:1; 18:10-14;
Romans 8:26*

OPENING PRAYER: Our Father in Heaven: We are thankful that we are your children, created in your image for a close relationship with you. In prayer, we can talk with you frankly, heart-to-heart. We can say anything, ask for anything, trusting your wise love to give us what we really need. Sometimes we do not know what to say to you; words fail us. However, you always listen with loving concern. Send now your Holy Spirit to teach us how to pray as we ought. Jesus knew how to pray, and gave us these words to use when we pray together, saying The Lord's Prayer . . . .

LESSON: Today we continue our study of Jesus' teachings on prayer. We begin with a confession of Paul, one most of us probably can make: "For we do not know how to pray as we ought, but [the] Spirit intercedes with sighs too deep for words" (Romans 8:26). Sometimes we do not know how to tell God what is in our minds, on our hearts, and on our consciences. We struggle hard to put our concerns into words.

However, Paul assures us that God's Holy Spirit is always here to help us. How? The Spirit may put words in our minds and on our lips. The Spirit may tell the Father what we are trying to say. The Spirit may remind us of ways Jesus set an example for us, or of what he taught us.

We now look at a few Bible passages, beginning with a request by his disciples: "Lord, teach us to pray" (Luke 11:1). Part of his answer was the Lord's Prayer, the subject of our last lesson. Jesus also taught that prayer should be private—between the individual and God. **(Read Matthew 6:5-8.)** Jesus' behavior, as well as his teaching, emphasized the private and personal nature of prayer.

The New Testament frequently reports that Jesus went off alone to pray: "Many crowds would gather to hear him. . . . But he would withdraw to deserted places and pray" (Luke 5:15*b*-16). "In the morning, while it was still very dark, he got up and went out to a deserted place, and there he prayed" (Mark 1:35).

It seems clear that Jesus favored private over public prayer. Even during synagogue worship, he cautioned that one should pray from the proper motives. He emphasized humility and simplicity. A lot of fancy words are not needed or appropriate, as the Lord's Prayer itself demonstrates. We have seen how much it says in a few simple phrases.

One of the most important things Jesus taught us about prayer is to pray humbly. Remember his parable about the Pharisee and the tax collector who came to the Temple to pray (Luke 18:10-14). The first thanked God that he was a good, respected church leader, better than other people, such as this despised tax collector. The latter bowed low and said only, "God, be merciful to me, a sinner" (v. 13). Jesus declared that only the tax collector went home on a friendly basis with God, "for all who exalt themselves will be humbled, but all who humble themselves will be exalted" (v. 14).

The best example of humble prayer occurred when Jesus was in the Garden of Gethsemane, the night before he was to be crucified. Three times he begged God to spare him the Cross. Three times he said, "Not what I want but what you want" (Matthew 26:39). To pray humbly is to pray trusting God. It means putting yourself, your life, completely in God's hands, trusting his everlasting arms to take care of you, to bear you up—now and forever.

CLOSING PRAYER: Father: We are grateful that in prayer we can have a personal, heart-to-heart talk with you. We do not always know exactly what to say. Our hearts sigh and groan, but the words do not come. Please, Father, send your Holy Spirit, and teach us how to pray. In Jesus' name we ask this. Amen.

Questions for Reflection or Discussion

1. Do you sometimes feel that you do not "know how to pray as [you] ought"? Have you experienced help from the Holy Spirit? If so, in what ways?

2. Do these examples and teachings of Jesus relate to political discussions about prayer in schools and other public places? If so, how? If not, why?

3. Think of prayers you have heard at football games, legislatures, chamber of commerce banquets, and so forth. To what extent did they or didn't they fit Jesus' instructions about prayer? What criteria should be used in making that judgment?

4. Describe some examples of humble and of prideful prayers, from your own prayer life or from prayers you have heard. What are the earmarks of humble private prayer? Of humble public prayer?

5. Can we trust God as Jesus did—even if we receive the kind of response that Jesus got to his Gethsemane prayer?

37
Pray Urgently,
But Humbly

Mark 14:32-36; Luke 11:5-8; 18:1-5, 9-14

OPENING PRAYER: Dear Heavenly Father: We are thankful for all your many gifts to us. You have given us life—and family and friends to share it. All around us are people ready and able to help us meet our daily needs. Your greatest gift, however, was Jesus, your Son and our Savior. He shared our joys and sorrows, our temptations, our pains, and finally our death. Then, as the Christ, he rose to new life, abundant eternal life with you. By dying, he saved us to join him in the heavenly kingdom, to be at home with you. We remember all he did for us, and we are thankful. We also remember the words he gave us to use when we pray together, saying The Lord's Prayer . . . .

LESSON: One of the main things Jesus taught his disciples was how to pray. Prayer was an important part of his life, an important part of his relationship with the Father. Prayer can be a very important part of our relationship with God, who is our Father, too. The Lord's Prayer, which we have already studied, can be a model for all our praying. However, there are many other ways in which Jesus, by parables and his own behavior, taught us how to pray.

Our temptation is to pray for what we *want,* rather than what we *need.* God knows that some of the things we want are impossible, and others would even be bad for us. God gives us what he knows is best. However, in Jesus, he also tells us that it is perfectly all right to ask him for what we want—even to keep asking again and again. We learn that from two of Jesus' parables.

127

(Read Luke 11:5-8.) In Jesus' day, most people traveled slowly by foot or on a donkey, over dusty roads. They would drop in unexpectedly on friends or family for some food or a night's rest. You would give them some water to drink and wash up a little, then you would feed them. Imagine a man showing up at midnight and there is no bread in the house.

So, you run next door and knock until the neighbor calls out sleepily, "Who's there?"

You ask to borrow three loaves of bread.

"No way," he says, "Get lost! You're waking up the kids."

Jesus said, "Keep asking and asking; be persistent. He will get up eventually and give you whatever you need." That is, God will give you what you *need*. Not all you want or all you ask for. Not peanut butter and jelly to go on the bread. Just what you actually need. Do not be ashamed, Jesus said, to keep on asking—especially, if like this man, you are asking for something to give to someone else.

(Read Luke 18:1-5.) The widow kept "dogging" the judge. She came to the courthouse; followed him on the street; phoned him at home, asking and asking for what she wanted. Wouldn't you say that she was obnoxious? Worn down, finally the judge gave in. Did Jesus mean that God is an unfriendly, arbitrary judge, who helps us just to get us off his back? Not at all! He was simply driving home the point that it is all right to be persistent, to keep on asking for what we want. It is OK to pray urgently, even aggressively. Sooner or later, God will act. But, remember: It may not be in the way we wanted.

Finally, we can learn from Jesus' own urgent prayer in the Garden of Gethsemane. **(Read Mark 14:32-36.)** Three times Jesus begged in anguish. Three times he pleaded for what he wanted. All three times, he ended, "Not what I want, but what you want" (v. 36). We can learn two things about prayer from this. First, as the parables taught, it is all right to keep asking God urgently for what we want. Second, we must always trust God to decide the future. We should pray while trusting God's wisdom and love. That is, we should be humble.

The previous lesson touched briefly on the parable about a Pharisee and a publican praying in the Temple. To get the full meaning, some facts are helpful. To us, Pharisee is a bad name. Actually, the Pharisees were devoted religious laymen, practicing their religion faithfully, as they understood it. They were not priests, just the leaders in their congregations.

A publican was a Jew working as a tax collector for the hated Roman army of occupation. Many of them squeezed out all the money they could, gave the Romans only what they had to, and kept the rest for themselves. No wonder they were considered both traitors and sinners, despised and shunned by their fellow Jews.

Jesus used these two familiar types to make a point about how to pray. **(Read Luke 18:9-14.)** When we pray, we must recognize our faults and the limits of our understanding. We must be humble. We pray humbly, leave the final decision to God, and accept whatever he gives us with a thankful heart.

CLOSING PRAYER: O God, our Heavenly Father: We are thankful that as your children, we can talk with you in prayer, telling you everything that is in our hearts and on our minds. We can trust your fatherly love to give us what is best for us. Help us to pray freely and completely. Even when we pray urgently, help us to pray humbly, trusting you in all things. We ask this in Jesus' name. Amen.

Questions for Reflection or Discussion

1. Do most people you know ask God for things they really need? Do you? Why or why not?
2. Do you believe that it is all right to ask God, and keep on asking him, for anything you want? If so, how is that related to the way you think about and relate to him?
3. What do you have to think, feel, and say, in order to pray both urgently and humbly?
4. Remember the tax collector's prayer (Luke 18:13-14). Do you identify with him, or with the Pharisee? How could the tax collector leave more "justified," more reconciled to God, than the other man?

129

38
Messiah:
A Suffering Servant

Luke 4:14-21; Isaiah 52:13–53:12; Mark 10:32-34

OPENING PRAYER: Our Father: We are thankful for this new day
you have given us. You, LORD, are the Creator of all that exists.
You are the Lord of all seasons. You are with us all the year, look-
ing after us. You are with us in our winters as well as our springs.
We are thankful, O LORD, for all you do for us; for your steadfast
love, especially as it is revealed in Jesus: Jesus the Babe of
Bethlehem and Christ who died on the Cross to save us; the
Resurrected Lord who leads us into eternal life. Therefore,
together we pray the words he taught us, saying The Lord's
Prayer . . . .

LESSON: We now begin several lessons on the last days of Jesus'
earthly life. The purpose is to understand his suffering and death
more completely, and thus be properly grateful for his sacrificial
love. We seek the deep meaning of his Crucifixion and
Resurrection, its meaning for us personally. We will follow him
on his last journey from safety in Galilee to danger in Jerusalem,
watch his triumphal entry into the city, and discover beyond the
Hosannas a gathering storm. As the end approaches, we will see
him at a Last Supper and in anguished prayer in the Garden;
then we will hear his words from the Cross. The climax of what
we call Holy Week is the happy discovery of an Empty Tomb.
For centuries, the weeks before Easter have been set aside by the
Church for a period of study and reflection called Lent.

We begin with the bitter question faced by Jesus' disciples after his death: Why? Why did the Messiah have to die? Did Jesus really have to suffer a painful death on the Cross? What is a Messiah, anyway? The disciples were puzzled. The One they thought had come to save had himself been crucified. They saw not power, but weakness. Does that puzzle us, too? The disciples searched Scripture for answers; so must we. They found some answers in the book of Isaiah, which Jesus knew well. Its ideas influenced the way he defined and carried out his ministry. Some of the disciples remembered that he had announced his ministry to his home synagogue in Nazareth by quoting Isaiah 61:1-2. **(Read Luke 4:14-21.)**

Other passages in Isaiah are even more important in helping us understand Jesus' last days, his journey to the Cross. They are called the Suffering Servant passages. They describe a person who lives for others, suffers for others, dies for others. Jesus knew what the prophet had said, and it helped him become God's Man for Others, rather than the expected political/military Messiah. He entered Jerusalem not as a military hero but as Prince of Peace; not on a prancing white war horse, but on a donkey's plodding colt.

(Read Isaiah 52:13–53:12.) The prophets spoke and wrote in poetry. Poetry communicates in symbols, figures of speech. And here we find images that describe the suffering and death of Jesus; that describe what the Cross means to us; that communicate how little we deserve God's forgiving love. They suggest how grateful we should be. The main image is that of Paschal Lamb, the Lamb of God who "willingly gave his life . . . [to take] the place of many sinners" (53:12d GNB); who "was wounded for our transgressions, crushed for our iniquities; . . . and by his bruises we are healed" (53:5).

These words help us remember and, in a small way, understand what Jesus did for us. They teach that love which suffers for others is more powerful than war horses or atom bombs. Love, not violence, is God's Way. Love is the Power that saves. For good reason, we call Jesus the Prince of Peace.

As Jesus walked toward Jerusalem, he realized what was coming, but his disciples did not understand. **(Read Mark 10:32-**

34.) Jesus knew, and went anyway. In the lessons that follow, we will go with him from Galilee to Golgotha. We will attempt to understand how and why he suffered and died for us. The more we understand, the better we are prepared to accept the joy and hope of a resurrected life, the gift of Easter.

CLOSING PRAYER: Heavenly Father: Help us use our study of Jesus' suffering and death to become better Christians—not only better able to receive the gift of salvation, but also better able to share his way of life, a life lived for others. Help us to learn from our study of the end of his earthly life; his suffering, death, and resurrection. For these things, and for him, we give you thanks. Amen.

Questions for Reflection or Discussion

1. The passages from Mark and Luke present two different aspects of Jesus' ministry. How would you describe them? Did they conflict, or were they complementary?
2. Put into your own words the prophet's poetic description of the Suffering Servant. Did making that "translation" help you better understand Jesus as Messiah?
3. Is suffering necessary to serve other persons? To serve God? Why, or why not? Give examples from your life or that of others you know well.
4. Imagine you were going to Jerusalem with Jesus and heard him tell what was going to happen there. What were you and the other disciples thinking and saying to each other? What did you think Jesus was thinking and feeling as you approached Jerusalem?

39
On to Jerusalem!

Luke 9:51; 17:11-13; 18:15-16, 31-34; 19:1-10; John 11:1-43

OPENING PRAYER: Our Heavenly Father: we come together again, thankful for your many blessings—especially for your gift of life in Jesus Christ our Lord. He came to earth in human flesh and blood; served his people the Jews; then suffered and died for *all* your children. We are thankful that, after the cold of winter, spring comes with its greening fields, flowers and singing birds; with new life and growth, with the promise of harvest to come. The death of winter is always followed by the rebirth of spring. Today we remember how Jesus went toward the Cross, and how he died there before being raised up to new life with you. We pray together, using the words he taught us, saying The Lord's Prayer . . . .

LESSON: Our study of Jesus' last days on earth can bring us sadness, yet it also fills us with expectation. We follow him as he traveled from Galilee to Jerusalem, knowing that he would be arrested, tried, and sentenced to death on a Cross. Yet he went anyway; he went to die for our salvation. For us this is a time of preparation and recommitment; a time to examine and cleanse ourselves, to receive again and celebrate our new life in that Kingdom, made possible by Jesus' Crucifixion and Resurrection. We begin by reviewing one aspect of Jesus' life, and then following him on his last journey to Jerusalem.

From the beginning of his ministry, Jesus ran into trouble with religious and government authorities. Why? He interpreted legalistic religious regulations in the light of God's love. He emphasized the principles of love and justice. He cured people, even on the Sabbath. He challenged the teachings of the priests and Pharisees. He did not act as they thought a prophet should act, much less a Messiah. Almost from the beginning, they plotted to stop him by imprisoning or killing him.

However, he was very popular with the poor, the common people, especially the country people in Galilee. So Jesus was relatively safe out in the villages. Jerusalem was dangerous, but he went there fairly often and taught in the Temple. At night, however, Jesus went to Bethany, a nearby village where he had friends, especially Lazarus, Martha, and Mary. He often ate and spent the night in their home.

When the time came for Jesus to die, to have his final showdown with the authorities, "He steadfastly set his face to go to Jerusalem" (Luke 9:51 KJV), even though he knew what would happen there. He did not hurry, but walked the dusty roads with his followers, carrying on his usual ministry: teaching, preaching, healing, associating with all kinds of people. Luke's Gospel reports a number of specific events along the way. These events summarize Jesus' ministry and show how his actions revealed the love of God for all human beings.

"As Jesus made his way to Jerusalem . . . along the border between Samaria and Galilee. . . . [H]e was met by ten men suffering from a dreaded skin disease. They stood at a distance and shouted, 'Jesus! Master! Have pity on us!'" (Luke 17:11-13 GNB). Lepers were considered loathsome persons and were feared. No one would asociate with them. Jesus did, and he healed all ten of them. But only one, a foreigner, came back to thank him.

"Some people brought their babies to Jesus for him to place his hands on them. The disciples . . . scolded them . . . but Jesus called the children to him and said, 'Let the children come to me and do not stop them, because the Kingdom of God belongs to such as these'" (Luke 18:15-16 GNB).

Luke reports (19:1-7) that as Jesus went through Jericho, he had dinner in the home of a "chief tax collector" named Zacchaeus. Now, all tax collectors were considered sinners and traitors. They forced the Jews to pay taxes to the Roman government. This Zacchaeus was a *chief* tax collector, one of the worst. Luke says that "Zacchaeus . . . welcomed him with great joy"

(v. 6 GNB). However, "All the people who saw it started grumbling, 'This man has gone as a guest to the home of a sinner!'" (v. 7 GNB).

John reports (11:1-43) a special event toward the end of the journey. Lazarus, Jesus' close friend in Bethany, fell sick unto death. His sisters sent a messenger to Jesus saying, "Please hurry here and heal our brother." Despite their close friendship, Jesus continued his journey, teaching, preaching, and healing as he went. His God-given mission came first. When he reached Bethany, Lazarus was dead and buried.

"Jesus wept," showing his human love and compassion. Then he showed his divine power over death. Standing in the sunshine among Lazarus' friends and neighbors, Jesus shouted down into the dark smelly grave, "Lazarus, come out!" And Lazarus came out into the sunshine of life with Jesus.

(Read Luke 18:31-34.) On this last journey to Jerusalem, Jesus knew he would suffer and die. The Twelve and other disciples were with him, but they did not understand what was ahead. In one sense, he walked alone. As he went, Jesus continued the ministry to which God had called him, preaching and teaching. He associated with rich and poor; Jews and foreigners; lepers and other outcasts; sinners and hated Roman stooges. He showed his love for all, even the "least of these," the little children. In the next lesson, we will follow Jesus into the city.

CLOSING PRAYER: O God, Father of our Lord Jesus Christ: We are thankful for your gift of life—Life Eternal—given us through the suffering, death, and resurrection of Jesus. As we try to share the last days and hours of his earthly life, help us to be truly thankful for this great gift of love; and to feel closer to him and to you. Praise the LORD! Amen.

Questions for Reflection or Discussion

1. Jesus was "steadfast" in his determination to follow God's way to the Cross. Note examples of this during his journey from Galilee to Jerusalem. Does his behavior strengthen

your determination to be steadfast and faithful to him and his way? How?

2. When Jesus blessed the children, he said that childlike qualities were required for entering the Kingdom. What are these qualities that we adults should try to have? Which of these qualities come easily for you? Which do you need help in "practicing"?

3. Another time when Jesus healed a leper, he did it by actually touching a man that people did not even want to get close to. What people in your community do most residents try to avoid? What about their bodies and/or behavior is the basis of this attitude? How does Jesus want us to think about and treat such people?

4. Jesus wept when his friend Lazarus died. What does this tell you about Jesus? Does this help you when you face grief? How?

40
Triumphal Entry
Into Gathering Storm

Mark 11:1-11, 15-19; 12:13-17, 28-31; 14:1-2, 10-11

OPENING PRAYER: O God, Father of our Lord Jesus Christ: We are thankful for your love and for the care you give us. You are with us every day. Your everlasting arms are always ready to hold us, to lift us up when we call on you for help. We are especially thankful for your love revealed in Jesus—revealed in his ministry and in his suffering and painful death on the Cross for our salvation. Help us to follow him through the events and experiences of his last days. Help us to understand more fully the gift of the Crucifixion and Resurrection. Now we pray together, using the words he taught us, saying The Lord's Prayer . . . . .

LESSON: We continue to follow Jesus through his last days on earth. In the previous lesson, we left Jesus in the village of Bethany, just outside Jerusalem. He spent the night there, after calling his friend Lazarus from a dark tomb back to life.

The city of Jerusalem was full of excited visitors preparing for the Passover. This was the main Jewish religious festival. Passover was, and still is, the time when Jews remember and celebrate the way God saved their ancestors, slaves in Egypt, and led them into a Promised Land. Jerusalem was full of pilgrims. Jews had come from all over Judea, and, like Jesus, down from Galilee. Many had come from other countries.

It was a time of excitement, celebration, expectation. Many people hoped to hear Jesus preach at the Temple. Most were hoping for a Messiah to come, one who would free the country from the Roman army of occupation and establish a Jewish kingdom of peace, prosperity, and freedom. However, Jesus was not the kind of Messiah most people expected. He taught love, compassion, forgiveness, justice. He taught loyalty to God the Father in Heaven, not to the political and religious authorities.

Mark describes Jesus' triumphal entry into a gathering storm. **(Read Mark 11:1-11, 15-19.)** The crowds hailed him. Many thought him the Messiah, even though he had no soldiers and was riding on a little donkey. Soon, however, he was in trouble with the authorities, beginning with his cleansing of the Temple.

Each evening, he went to spend the night in the relative safety of Bethany. Each morning, he came back into the city to teach in the Temple. The leaders listened to what he said and asked trick questions. They tried to trap him into saying something against their religion, or against either the Jewish or the Roman governments. **(Read Mark 12:13-17, 28-31.)** With wise answers and quotations from Scripture, Jesus avoided their traps. However, that made them even more angry, more afraid of him.

As the day of the Passover feast came closer, the authorities grew even more determined to eliminate this man. To the people generally, he was a popular teacher (Rabbi) and prophet. To the authorities, he was a dangerous troublemaker. **(Read Mark 14:1-2, 10-11.)** The trap was now laid, waiting to be sprung. That was to happen Thursday night after the Last Supper, when Jesus and the Twelve ate the Passover meal together in an upstairs room. The next lesson will begin there.

CLOSING PRAYER: Father: As we look toward the Cross, and beyond it to the Resurrection, help us to look into our own minds and hearts. Help us to measure our understanding of Jesus as the revelation of your forgiving, saving love. Is our knowledge and understanding of Jesus great enough for us to be truly grateful for his saving grace? We thank you, Father, because you loved us enough to send your Son Jesus to suffer and die for us, to be our Savior. Amen.

Questions for Reflection or Discussion

1. Although Jesus did not come as a military hero, he was greeted with great excitement by many. What things about

his person and behavior should we still find exciting? How does he excite *you*?

2. Exactly why did the Temple need cleansing? What worldly things come between us and God? In the Church? In private prayer? In daily life?

3. Can you think of trick or misleading questions now being directed to people who are sincerely and humbly trying to follow the Jesus revealed in the Bible? Could you use prayerful reading of the New Testament to answer them? Give one or two examples.

4. Why do *you* think Judas Iscariot went to the chief priests and plotted to betray Jesus to them? Is that a clue to motives we should avoid?

41

A Last Supper and the Cross

Mark 14:12–15:4

OPENING PRAYER: We are thankful, Father, for the spring that follows winter. We are thankful for warmth and rest, for sunshine and rebirth. We are especially thankful, O LORD, for your love, which brings new life with its promises of growth and harvest. We are even more thankful, Father, for Jesus Christ, our Lord and Savior. It is through him that we receive your loving gift of abundant, eternal life with you. With grateful hearts, we pray together, using the words Jesus taught us, saying The Lord's Prayer . . . .

LESSON: We have followed Jesus almost to the end of his earthly life. Our attempt to understand more completely the meaning of his suffering, death, and resurrection is approaching its climax.

On Thursday evening of Holy Week, we celebrate the Feast of Unleavened Bread with which Jesus began Passover. At this holy, joyful time, Jews remember how God led their ancestors out of slavery in Egypt. That Last Supper of Jesus should have been a time of relaxed, solemn joy. Instead, it was a confused time. The Twelve did not understand what was happening, just that something threatened. Jesus knew; and he knew that one of them would betray him. Selected verses from Mark's Gospel cover the main events of the Last Supper, his agonized prayers in the garden, and the all-night trial before the priestly High Council. Early Friday morning, he was taken before the Roman governor Pilate; was nailed to the rugged Cross on Golgotha; died in the middle of the afternoon; then was buried hurriedly before the Sabbath began at sundown. **(Read Mark 14:12–15:4.)**

That was late Friday afternoon. Do you remember Jesus'

dying cry? "My God! My God! Why have you forsaken me?" This is the first verse of Psalm 22. Jesus knew the psalm, and in the throes of painful human death, he remembered it. It expressed what he was feeling. His anguished cry, as much as anything in the Bible, is proof that Jesus really shared our human life, including the physical and emotional agony of death. He knows and understands us because he shared our humanness.

Today we call that day Good Friday. For his disciples, it was a dark, sad day. They had to wait three days for the Easter answer to their question, "What do we do now?" We, too, wait for Easter. Unlike them, we wait in hope, for we have heard already the Good News from that Empty Tomb.

CLOSING PRAYER: O God: We are thankful for that first Good Friday; thankful that your son Jesus was so full of divine love that he was willing to suffer on the Cross and die a painful death, even for me. Fill us with your love and with secure hope in our abundant, eternal life with you. In Jesus' name we pray. Amen.

Questions for Reflection or Discussion

1. Recall a celebration of the Lord's Supper that had special meaning for you. What made it so special? Read the accounts in Matthew 26:26-30, Mark 14:22-25, and Luke 22:17-20. Which words of Jesus about the gift of Bread and Wine are most meaningful to you?
2. What can Jesus' prayer in the Garden teach us about prayer, about our relation to God the Father, and about Christian discipleship?
3. What do we learn from Pilate, the Roman governor (Mark 15:1-15)? When do we "wash our hands"? By what actions are we tempted "to satisfy the crowd"?
4. Peter denied he knew Jesus three times. In what ways do our words and actions "say" to others that we do not know Jesus and his way of life? What can we learn from the fact that Peter later became a brave leader in the Christian movement?

42
Cry of Anguish/Hymn of Praise

Psalm 22; Mark 15:34, 37

OPENING PRAYER: O God, our Father in Heaven: We are thankful to be alive on this new day and to be gathered together in your name to study your Word in Scripture. Sometimes we are discouraged; in our despair, we cry out, as Jesus did, "My God, why have you forsaken me?" Yet, deep inside we know, as Jesus did, that you have not forsaken us. You are right here with us all the time, walking beside us to the very end. We are thankful that we can reach out and feel the support of your Presence. And, Father, we are thankful for Jesus, your Son and our Savior, who taught us to pray together, saying The Lord's Prayer . . . .

LESSON: This lesson focuses on Jesus' last, dying word from the Cross. Mark reports that Jesus cried out in a loud voice: "'My God, my God, why have you forsaken me?' . . . Then Jesus gave a loud cry and breathed his last" (15:34*b*, 37). This cry of anguish is the first verse of Psalm 22. Both Jesus and his disciples knew this psalm well. What was he saying to his followers who stood around the Cross? They knew the whole psalm by heart. What is he saying to us today?

Key verses summarize the psalm's message. **(Read Psalm 22:1-2, 9-11, 14-15, 19, 27-31.)** Why did Jesus, Son of God, Divinity in the flesh, cry out in anguished despair, "My God, why have you forsaken me?" It doesn't seem right, does it? Actually, it tells us a lot about God, about Jesus as Savior, and about God's plan for our salvation. To understand, we must remember that the Bible says, and the Church teaches, that Jesus was completely human as well as fully divine. This is one of the holy mysteries of Christian belief. We accept it in our hearts by faith.

In God's plan, if Jesus was to be God's suffering servant and our Savior (see lesson 38), he had to take our place on the Cross and die for us. To substitute for us, he had to share fully in our human condition. He had to go through what we go through, experience what we experience. Separation from God is a consequence of Sin, and Jesus bore all our sin on the Cross. It was as a fellow human being that he died a painful death for our sin. Dying and in physical pain, Jesus knew, if only for an instant, our feeling of being forsaken by everyone, even God. We feel that way at times; it is only human. Jesus was both completely human and fully divine.

However, that is not all his dying cry tells us. Jesus and his followers knew the whole psalm. It begins with that cry of anguish, expressing deep despair: "I have cried desperately for help, but still it does not come. . . . All my bones are out of joint . . . my tongue sticks to the roof of my mouth" (Psalm 22:1*b*, 14*b*, 15*b* GNB). Then there was a cry for help: "O LORD, don't stay away from me! Come quickly to my rescue!" (v. 19 GNB).

The psalm ends, however, with praise to the glory of the LORD, who has the power to save; the God of all peoples, in all places, at all times: "All nations will remember the LORD. . . . The LORD is king. . . . Future generations will serve him. . . . People not yet born will be told: 'The LORD saved his people'" (vv. 27*a*, 28*a*, 30*a*, 31 GNB).

Jesus knew human despair. At the same time, he knew that the whole psalm was known to his followers, including the confident hymn of praise with which it ends. Thus he communicated to them his supreme confidence in God, his Father. He tells us, through Mark's Gospel, of his complete trust in God, our Father. He is confident that each generation of his followers will tell the next that "The LORD saved his people." From the Cross, Jesus used this psalm to proclaim the glory and the saving power of God "to people not yet born." That's us! We *have* heard the Good News! Thanks be to God!

CLOSING PRAYER: Heavenly Father: We, too, get discouraged and know despair. We, too, cry out for your help. Yet we have learned from Jesus that we can have faith in you, confident that you are the God who created us, who loves us, who is always close and ready to help us. Send now your Holy Spirit to strengthen us in the sure knowledge that you are the LORD who saves his people. Amen.

Questions for Reflection or Discussion

1. Have you ever felt abandoned by God? If so, what helped you deal with the experience? If not, what resources have helped you escape such experiences?
2. Can you believe that Jesus felt abandoned by God? Why or why not?
3. It is difficult to believe that our Savior was human as well as divine. Remembering Jesus' last days (lessons 39–42), what specific things remind you of his humanity? Of his Divinity?
4. From studying this psalm, do you have a new appreciation, a deepened faith, about Jesus' last moments on the Cross? What new insights have you gained?

43
Easter:
The Empty Tomb

Mark 16:1-8; Matthew 28:1-8; Luke 24:1-12; John 20:1-18

OPENING PRAYER: Eternal God, our Father: We are thankful for the saving love which you and Jesus showed for us in his suffering, death, and resurrection. By his death, we die to sin. Through his resurrection, we are shown the way to life, abundant eternal life with you. Help us to live each day in this Easter joy, this Easter hope. We *can* live in hope and faith because you are with us in joy and sorrow, in our pain and fear. And you are with us in death, bearing us up in your everlasting arms and carrying us to live with you in your heavenly home. Therefore, we pray together the words Jesus taught us, saying The Lord's Prayer . . . .

LESSON: We come now to the joyful Easter climax of the lessons on Jesus' last days on earth. We have prepared by trying to understand better and appreciate more fully the last days of his earthly life.

After Jesus' death, deep despair filled the disciples who had walked from Galilee with him. Their joy, their high hopes on Palm Sunday, were in the dust. Friday night, all day Saturday, and Saturday night they huddled together, wondering: "What will we do with our lives now? He is gone, what future do we have?" They had believed he would throw out the Roman army; but its soldiers had killed him. They thought he would establish a kingdom of freedom, love, and justice; but the same old rulers were still in power. He was dead and buried.

Saturday night, they still were in the clutch of death, saying, "There is no tomorrow for us." Tomorrow was Sunday, the first day of the week. It was to be Easter Sunday, the first tomorrow of a new era for them, and for all humankind. They did not know that—yet. All four Gospels report what was revealed Sunday morning. It may be instructive to read them all, beginning with Mark, the earliest written, and ending with John, written perhaps sixty years later.

(Read Mark 16:1-18; Matthew 28:1-8; Luke 24:1-12; John 20:1-18.) That is one of the most wonderful, exciting stories ever told; the best Good News human beings have ever heard. Note that women were the first to hear an angel announce the Good News. These reports from the empty tomb indicate that women were among his most loving and devoted followers. "They helped him," the Scripture says. They came, in sadness and despair, to perform one last service of love—to anoint his dead body. They were at the head of the line to hear the Good News.

Note also that the four reports differ in a few details. Is that important to us? No, because they all agree on one significant fact: The tomb was empty, and an angel announced, "Jesus is not here, he is risen from the dead." Why the differences? The reports were written many years later. Only one of the writers, John, was an eyewitness; and he got there late. We also know that eyewitnesses give different reports of the same event. The more surprising and exciting the event, the greater the differences. And this was a miracle—a stupendous, mind-boggling miracle! Human minds cannot understand such an event and report it in "down-to-earth" terms. We just accept it in our hearts.

The angel reported, "He is not here; he is risen. Go and tell." Go tell the disciples. The women told, and the disciples believed—some more slowly than others. It transformed them! It transformed people lost in grief and uncertainty into strong, courageous, determined proclaimers of the Good News. They went out to tell all peoples and nations what was "the old, old story" by the time it got to us. We, too, can be transformed. We, too, can be sure that in Jesus, we have the Risen Lord. We, too, can be strong and brave as we follow him.

Early Christians had a greeting which they used with others. It was a kind of secret password, for it was dangerous to be a

Christian. It was also a proclamation. The greeting: "The Lord is risen!" If the stranger was not a Christian, he or she would just be puzzled; and the Christian was safe. A fellow Christian, however, would respond joyfully, "He is risen indeed!" Then they knew they were brothers and sisters in the faith. Unfortunately, most Christians have lost this joyful greeting, this proclamation of our faith—even on Easter Sunday. Perhaps if we revived it, we could recapture some of the joy and excitement of Jesus' early followers. In your Sunday school class, in church, or just with family or friends, you could say, "The Lord is risen," and coach them to reply, "He is risen indeed."

Shall we do that ourselves, right now? Will you join me?

"The Lord is risen!" "He is risen indeed!"

CLOSING PRAYER: Father: We thank you for your Easter love; for its joyful promise of abundant, eternal life. Help us to keep this faith and this hope alive in our hearts—always. In the name of Jesus, our Risen Lord, we pray. Alleluia! Amen.

Questions for Reflection or Discussion

1. Recall an Easter celebration that had special significance for you. Why was it more moving, joyful, inspiring than others? What particular thoughts and feelings did it evoke in you?
2. If you read all four accounts of the empty tomb, which means the most to you? Why? Which means the least? Why?
3. Have you ever been in a worship service or other setting in which the traditional Easter Greeting was used? If so, what were your reactions? Whether you have shared it before or not, would you like to see its use revived? In what settings (e.g., worship service, small group, family, other)?
4. Part of the joy of Easter is expressed in its music. What are your favorite Easter hymns? Why not sing them now!

44

The Church Is Born

Acts 1:4–2:47

OPENING PRAYER: O Lord, our God: You are Lord of everything that exists. You created the universe; its earth and sky and seas; its plants and animals. You created us, male and female, in your own image. You were with us in our childhood and in our middle years. Now that we are old, you are still with us—even in our aches and pains. You are especially close to us in our fears, even our fear of death. Help us, Father, to remember that you are the Lord of Life who conquered death. We are thankful that death is a door you open so that we can spend eternal, abundant life with you. You are our God; nearer than hands and feet, now and forever; and we are thankful. Therefore, we pray together as Jesus taught us, saying The Lord's Prayer . . . .

LESSON: This lesson is about a day of celebration for all Christians, the birthday of the Church. It was called Pentecost because it came fifty days after the first Easter, the Day of Resurrection.

(**Read Acts 1:4-14.**) With Jesus gone, his followers were still asking, "What do we do now?" They were waiting, but now they had Jesus' promise that something very important was about to happen. But what? They were not sure. The eleven disciples selected Matthias, a fellow believer from Galilee, to replace Judas Iscariot and join them in witness to Jesus. Their inner circle of twelve was complete again, surrounded by more than one hundred other believers, both women and men. All of them were still marking time, still waiting for something. It came on the Day of Pentecost.

(**Read Acts 2:1-13.**) Something very special had happened. The disciples were excited, stimulated, energized in unusual ways. A crowd of outsiders had gathered to see what was going on, but were puzzled. Some thought, from the unusual behavior, that the disciples were drunk. Then Peter stood up to explain what had happened. He said that it was too early in the morning for anyone to be drunk on the weak new wine. Then he quoted Scripture, interpreting words from the prophet Joel as predicting this event. He concluded by proclaiming Jesus as the Messiah, the Risen Lord.

(**Read Acts 2:14-24; 32–33; 36-41.**) Peter's sermon "cut to the heart" of many listeners, as he issued a call to repent and be baptized. About three thousand people answered his call. The Church of Jesus Christ had been born of the Holy Spirit, and it began to grow. Peter emerged as its first main leader. Those who had been uncertain, waiting, were now aflame with a message to share. At first it was shared mainly among themselves.

(**Read Acts 2:42-47.**) They were now a growing community of shalom, of peace and security. We, too, have been called into the Church of Jesus Christ; called to be his people, to be members of the Body of Christ still alive in the world.

CLOSING PRAYER: Father: You have given us many gifts, and we are thankful. We are especially grateful for the gift of Jesus Christ and his Church. With the flame of your Holy Spirit, you created the Church. It preaches the Good News of our salvation. It nurtures us in the Christian life. It does your work in the world. It shows us the open door to eternal, abundant life with you, here and in heaven. Thank you, LORD. Amen.

Questions for Reflection or Discussion

1. Even after Jesus' resurrection and ascension, his followers were still uncertain about what to do; they were marking time. Why? Are we—are you—ever like that? Why?
2. How did those followers feel after being "touched" by the Spirit at Pentecost? Have you, or people you know, ever felt like that? Describe the experience.

3. In the U.S. today, there are whole denominations, and movements within denominations (including "high churches" such as Episcopal and Catholic), which call themselves "Pentecostal." Would it be a good thing if all churches were like that? Why or why not?
4. The Pentecostal churches are the fastest growing Christian churches in the world. Why do you think this is so?
5. Think of the very close, sharing fellowship among those first "church members" as described in Acts 2:44-47. Would you like to see all church congregations live like that? Why or why not?
6. Can you imagine "sharing all things in common"? Since the days of the early Church, there have been Christian communities like the one described in Acts 2. Are there any now? Where? Should there be?

45
The Church:
Persecuted and Spreading

Mark 16:15; Matthew 28:20; Acts 2, 4, 6–12 Selections

OPENING PRAYER: "O Lord, our Lord, how excellent is thy Name in all the earth": Everything that exists is your creation. Sunshine falls on the hills. Birds fly in the air. Animals roam the prairie and the woodland. We are thankful for all of creation, our home. We are also thankful, Father, that you created us in your own image, capable of living in fellowship with you and with one another. We are especially grateful for our family and friends, and for all the people who are interested in us and want to help us. We are most thankful, Father, for your gift of Jesus Christ, your Son, our Savior. He has summoned us into his Church, the Body that is his continuing presence in the world. Therefore, we pray in his name as he taught us, saying The Lord's Prayer . . . .

LESSON: The experience of Pentecost created the Church of Jesus Christ. What was going on in those first little churches? They were persecuted for their beliefs and actions, and they spread the Good News of God's saving love in Christ. They responded to Jesus' final words just before his ascension: "Go into all the world and proclaim the good news to the whole creation" (Mark 16:15); "And remember, I am with you always" (Matthew 28:20).

However, they did not rush off as missionaries right away. **(Read Acts 2:42, 46-57.)** Things were peaceful; there was no trouble, no persecution—yet. That came very soon. Peter and John healed a man crippled from birth, and they did it *in the name of Jesus*. That greatly upset the authorities. **(Read Acts**

4:1-20.) Peter, John, and others kept right on telling about Jesus and speaking in his name. The persecution began in Jerusalem, but "the word of God continued to spread; the number of the disciples increased greatly in Jerusalem" (Acts 6:7).

Then the martyrdom of one believer sparked major trouble. (**Read Acts 6:8–7:2*a*; 7:51–8:3.**) "The apostles were scattered" (8:1), at first around Palestine, then far and wide. Everywhere they went, they preached the Good News of Jesus Christ. By scattering them, persecution aided the spread and growth of the Church. The apostles and other disciples were the first traveling evangelists. Originally they preached only to fellow Jews. Soon, however, they included converts to Judaism, and then Gentiles in general.

Philip rode in the chariot of an Ethiopian going back home, converted him, and baptized him in a stream beside the road (Acts 8:26-39). Peter had a compelling dream which opened up the Gentile world to him. It directed him to the home of a Roman army captain. (**Read Acts 10:9-48.**) Back in Jerusalem, members of the mother church were skeptical. They had been raised to have nothing to do with Gentiles. When Peter returned, he told them about his dream and about the gift of the Spirit to the converts. (**Read Acts 11:17-18.**)

Some early Christian missionaries went into Africa; others crossed Asia to India. The book of Acts, however, concentrates on the spread into Europe—in *our* direction. One man dominated that mission.

Saul, the young Pharisee who helped stone Stephen, became a major persecutor of the Church. However, Jesus met him on the road to Damascus and, as Paul, he became the major missionary of the early Christian movement. We know him as Saint Paul, author of many New Testament books. (**Read Acts 9:1-11, 17-20.**)

The remainder of the book of Acts concentrates on Paul and his associates. As you may guess, the church in Jerusalem was wary of Paul because of his past record, and because his plan to convert Gentiles was hard for them to accept. Finally, an agreement was reached. Paul was given a mission field away from Jerusalem:

north along the Mediterranean coast, including Turkey, Greece, Rome, and probably as far as Spain. Persecution followed Paul all the way. We last hear of him as a prisoner in Rome, where he probably died a martyr's death.

In summary, two things best describe events in the infant Church. First, it was persecuted. Its teachings called into question the way most people thought and behaved.

Second, it spread. Its members were missionaries. They preached to *all* kinds of people.

CLOSING PRAYER: Our Heavenly Father: We are thankful for your word in Scripture. Today you have helped us better understand the Church, which is your gift to us through your Son, Jesus Christ. You have called each of us to be a member. Help us to live with its rich gifts of fellowship, and of the peace that passes all understanding. Thank you, LORD. Amen.

Questions for Reflection or Discussion

1. The Church is not persecuted in the United States today. Why do you think that is so? Is it because we are doing everything right? Or is it because we are not like the early church? What, if anything, should we change?
2. Most members of the Jerusalem church felt uncomfortable about inviting Gentiles "into the fold." Are there groups whose presence in your congregation would make members "uncomfortable"? Who are they? What thoughts and feelings do you have about this?
3. Have you or someone you know had an experience which changed attitudes and behavior toward "outsiders," as Peter did? Like Saul/Paul? If so, what difference has it made in your/their life since then?
4. Do we think of ourselves as missionaries of the Christian church? If not, should we? How would this affect our behavior toward others? How would it affect society's reaction to the Church?

46
Called Out and Into Fellowship

*2 Timothy 1:9; 1 Peter 5:10; Romans 5:8; 8:28; Galatians 5:13;
Acts 2:44-47; 1 Corinthians 1:9*

OPENING PRAYER: O God our Father: In Heaven, your Name is holy to everyone. Everyone knows and lives by the rules of your Kingdom. Your will is done obediently by all. You want life on earth to be like that; and so do we. You have called us to be followers of Jesus Christ as members of his Church, living in fellowship with you and with one another. Send now your Holy Spirit to guide our hearts and minds as we study Scripture. Help us learn more about what it means to hear your call and say "yes" to a life in Christ. So we pray the words he taught us, saying The Lord's Prayer . . . .

LESSON: In previous lessons, we read about how the Church of Jesus Christ was born. *We* are the Church. This and the next lesson look at Scriptures which answer the question: What *is* the Church?

Today we will explore two main ways the Bible describes the nature and function of the Church, using the Greek words *ecclesia* and *koinonia*. *Ecclesia* means "called out," "summoned." It also applies to a group of people—a "congregation" or "church." The Church is made up of people who have been called away from "life as usual," called together into a community of faith in Jesus. We have promised to live, and to die, by that faith.

We have been summoned to live together in a special caring relationship with one another, with Jesus Christ, and with God the Father. *Koinonia* describes what that relationship is, or should be. It means living in community, in communion with one another, in fellowship. *Koinonia,* however, means a whole lot more than Sunday school class parties and covered-dish suppers. It refers to deep sharing, to caring about and taking care of one another. It means laughing, hurting, crying together. It means to be loving sisters and brothers in the family of God.

Most of the Scriptures that talk about this are from Paul's epistles and Luke's Acts of the Apostles. Among other questions, they ask, "What must we do to receive God's call into his Church?" The answer is: Nothing! He calls us because he loves us. All we need do is answer his summons; say "Yes" to God's invitation; accept his call. **(Read 2 Timothy 1:9.)** We do not need to be good or do good works. As Paul wrote, "While we still were sinners Christ died for us" (Romans 5:8). All we have to do is accept the Kingdom with thankful hearts. It is *then* that we are enabled to do "good works."

Peter also wrote about God's calls. **(Read 1 Peter 5:10.)** God's call is not just for now. It is eternal, forever. Once we are in the Church, God helps us to "move on toward perfection," as John Wesley, the founder of Methodism, once said. The Church gives us "firmness" and "strength" to live the Christian life. God's gifts include this sure promise: "We know that all things work together for good for those who love God, who are called according to his purpose" (Romans 8:28).

If the Church is to perform its ministries, both to its own members and to the world, then the members must live together in *koinonia*, in fellowship. Paul wrote: "My brothers [and sisters], you were called to be free. . . . [L]et love make you serve one another" (Galatians 5:13*a*, *c* GNB). We were freed *from* sin *for* a life of love and justice, where we treat all people justly and lovingly—starting with fellow church members who serve one another in love.

What does living in fellowship in the Church involve? The Jerusalem congregation after Pentecost practiced a close, total kind of *koinonia*. From time to time, some groups of Christians have tried to copy that model as Luke reported it. **(Read Acts 2:44-47.)** Today, only a few Christians try to live together like that. However, there *are* some specific everyday things we can do as we try to live in fellowship.

Suppose a member of your family, a member of your congregation, or a friend is on a mission project in Africa, or is stationed abroad in the military. How can you "be in fellowship" with this person? You can pray for and write to the person. If you can afford it, you can send money or mail some "goodies" not available there.

Suppose you know a young mother with a two-year-old and a brand new baby. She has her hands full and can do very little for anyone, except her own family. You can help her: Take a "covered dish" or offer babysitting to give her a morning or evening out.

Those who are homebound or residents in a home may have few ways to help those outside. But they can pray for others. They can smile at those around them. They can pat the shoulder or hold the hand of someone who is lonely or worried. We all know the kind words and kind deeds we would like to receive; we can say or do those same things for others. We can offer support over the phone as well as in person.

A final word comes from Saint Paul: "God is to be trusted, the God who called you to have fellowship with his Son Jesus Christ, our Lord" (1 Corinthians 1:9 GNB). That is part of the Good News we find all through the Bible: God is to be trusted; he is faithful to his promises. He is loving, faithful, dependable. "Trust God" is the main advice Scripture gives us. When we regularly trust our lives to God, we can live—and die—knowing that we are his children, whom he has called into eternal, abundant life with him in heaven.

CLOSING PRAYER: Father in Heaven: We are thankful that we can trust your love and care. You are with us to support us, to lift us up, to bring us home forever to the heavenly mansion with many rooms you have prepared for us. In Jesus' name we pray. Amen.

Questions for Reflection or Discussion

1. The Bible says that members of the Church have been "called." What do you understand by "call"? Called from what? To what?

2. Many church buildings have a "fellowship hall." Are the activities that go on there related to what the Bible called *koinonia*? Why or why not? Should they be?

3. Among the other things it does for us, the freeing gift of God's grace enables us to "serve one another." Yet we vary in skills, talents, and strength. Think of yourself and the other people around you. What are the things you *are* able to do to help and serve them as fellow children of God?

4. "God is to be trusted." Life is often full of problems, worries, uncertainties, fears, angers. Think of the ones that trouble you. Name those you have turned over to God. Which of the others can, and should, you trust God to take care of for you?

47

The Body of Christ in the World

Colossians 1:18; 3:12-15; 1 Corinthians 12:4-27; Ephesians 1:22-23; 4:4-16; Galatians 3:27-38; Romans 12:4-8

OPENING PRAYER: Dear Father: We are thankful for the Church of Jesus Christ. It brings us the Good News of your steadfast love, which forgives us and saves us through the death of Jesus on the Cross. We have heard and we accept the Good News from the empty tomb. Send now your Holy Spirit to help us learn more about your gift of life in the Church. Help us to live—and die—trusting in your gracious gift of strength and mercy. We ask this in Jesus' name, who taught us to pray together, saying The Lord's Prayer . . . .

LESSON: We continue our lessons on the Church. Today's focus is on the Church as the Body of Christ. Paul used the living, functioning human body as a symbol to illustrate an essential fact about the Church. The human body has many different parts, or "members"; all work together, in different ways, to make it function efficiently. Paul used this idea again and again in his letters: "[Christ] is the head of the body, the church" (Colossians 1:18); "[God] has put all things under [Christ's] feet and has made him the head over all things for the church, which is his body" (Ephesians 1:22-23).

A human body contains many different parts: head, hands, and feet; stomach, heart, and lungs. We call these limbs and organs "members" of the body. Men and women are the members—the limbs and organs of Christ's body, the Church. Paul wrote: "You are the body of Christ and individually members of

158

it" (1 Corinthians 12:27). Each person has his or her own place and function in the Church.

Paul made this point many times: "Just as in a single human body there are many limbs and organs, all with different functions, so all of us, united with Christ, form one body, serving individually as limbs and organs to one another" (Romans 12:4-5 NEB). Each person has unique talents and different strengths. Together, we form one dynamic unit dedicated to God's ministry in and to the world.

(Read 1 Corinthians 12:12-27.) Following each of the last two quotations, Paul lists the main functions being performed in those first Christian churches. We still have most of them in our own congregations: preach, teach, heal, encourage, serve, help, lead, administer, speak in tongues, interpret such speech. We may ask, What is the *purpose* of all these activities? **(Read 1 Corinthians 12:4-7.)** Everyone is to cooperate "for the common good." In another place, Paul says they are "for building up the body of Christ" (Ephesians 4:12). Each person is to do his or her own part, so that the whole Church functions effectively.

The Church has a dynamic unity. Paul emphasizes this unity, insisting on the equality of each person, each function. **(Read Galatians 3:27-28 and Ephesians 4:4-6.)** Paul frequently told the congregations about this unity in diversity—different "members" working together to build up the Church. **(Read Ephesians 4:7, 15-16.)** "When each separate part works as it should, the whole body grows" (v. 16c GNB). That sounds like *work*, does it not? And there *is* a lot of church work to be done. Some by the ordained ministers, but much by laypeople: teaching Sunday school, singing in the choir, cleaning up after covered-dish suppers, taking up the collection, running the finance drive, visiting and sending cards to those who are sick or grieving.

Some members can do few, perhaps none, of those things. What can those people do? Actually, we are called both to "do" and to "be." Here is one thing Paul said about that. **(Read Colossians 3:12-15.)** All members of the Church can strive to be kind, humble, gentle, forgiving, patient, loving. For many of us, *being* that kind of person is as hard as *doing* church *work!* However, you heard what God promised to persons like that: Peace—both now on earth and in heaven. Thank God for that!

CLOSING PRAYER: We are thankful, Father, that you love us and chose us for unity with Christ, with you, and with our fellow members in the Church. Please help us to be the kind of persons who build up the Body of Christ. In Jesus' name we pray. Amen.

Questions for Reflection or Discussion

1. In what way, or ways, does the idea of the Church as "the Body of Christ" apply to you personally?
2. The Bible says that each man and woman is given some talent or skill for "the common good," for "building up the church." When, and in what ways, have you done that? What is or was your "talent"? How do or did you use it?
3. Paul named things that we, especially as members of the Church, should "do" and "be." Is the "doing" or the "being" harder for you? Why? Of the things Paul asked us to be (Colossians 3:12-15), which is the easiest for you? The hardest? Why?
4. Are there other images for the Church that have meaning for you? If so, what?
5. What has the Church meant to you throughout your life?

48

Lazarus:
Called from Death to Life

John 11:1-44

OPENING PRAYER: We are thankful, O LORD, for this new day; and for your angels who guard us while we sleep. Sleep is like death: from sleep, too, we wake refreshed for a new life. Here we are, LORD, together again, seeking your Word in Scripture. Make us aware of your presence. Let your Holy Spirit open our minds and hearts to the Good News of the saving love of your Son, Jesus Christ, who taught us to pray together, saying The Lord's Prayer . . . .

LESSON: This is the last lesson on the Church of Jesus Christ. The Gospel of John tells how Jesus raised Lazarus, buried four days, from his grave. We find important teachings for us as individuals, and as members of the Church. We know this event as a miracle of God's power of life over death, working through Jesus. Here, however, we look at this gripping story in terms of the flesh-and-blood people involved, remembering that Jesus was the Word made flesh, completely human as well as fully divine.

When Jesus was in Jerusalem, he preached and healed in the Temple by day. He spent the night in the safety of Bethany, a village just outside the city. He had close friends there, a brother and two sisters: Lazarus, Mary, and Martha. Martha was a busy, hardworking housekeeper. She cooked, set the table, and prepared to feed Jesus and his disciples. Mary sat at his feet, drinking in every word. All we know about Lazarus is that he was sick, died, was buried, and then was called back to life.

(Read John 11:1-7, 17-22, 28-35, 38-44.) That's quite a story! Aside from the divine miracle, what Word is here for us?

1. Both sisters, were disappointed, even irritated, when he did not come. Mary was so disappointed, even angry, that she sulked in the house and did not come out until he asked for her.

2. When they came to the grave, no one wanted to face the facts or the smell of death; but Jesus said, "Roll back the stone."

3. Each of us has some grave in which we sleep, trapped away from the sunshine of life with other people, life with Jesus. Tombs of loneliness, fear, despair, perhaps anger, and almost certainly pain—physical, emotional, or both. Each of us needs to recognize any kind of darkness that surrounds us, the kind of grave clothes that tie us up. In some ways, it is quiet and comfortable in a grave; but dark and lonely, too.

4. Outside each dark cave, Jesus stands in the light among other people, among relationships, where there is life. Down into the darkness he shouts, "Lazarus, come out!" John, come out! Mary, come out! Whatever your name is, he is calling *you,* and me.

5. He does not come and *carry* us out. We have to do it ourselves—in the power of his love which, like a bright ray of sunshine, floods down into the darkness where we are.

6. And we come out: blinded, staggering toward his voice. Hands and feet still bound; face still behind a veil; we are not free of our problems—yet. We are moving toward the Light, toward him, toward family or friends, toward people ready to be friends, people ready to help us.

7. There is also a message here for those of us already standing in the sunshine of life with Jesus: "Roll back the stone"; and "Unbind him and let him go!" These words describe two responsibilities of the Church and its members.

The raising of Lazarus reveals the miraculous power of God's love over sin and death. It also tells each one of us, personally, to be aware of any spot of darkness in our lives, and then to hear the voice of Christ our Savior calling us to move out into the light of his love. First, we must decide to do that, even if that requires a struggle. Second, we should be aware of and welcome the people who are ready to help, holding out helping hands to help untie our bonds.

This Scripture also speaks to us as members of the Church. (a) We are told to "roll back the stone," to let sunshine into the darkness of someone's life. We are to help someone who is lonely, worried, afraid, angry, or in pain to move into the light of more abundant Christian life with family, friends, and helpers. (b) Also, we are to "untie" him or her. We are to help someone get rid of whatever idea, feeling, belief, memory, or pain is holding him or her back from fellowship with God and with others. These are two ways we can function as members of the Christian fellowship. There are many ways to roll back stones and untie shackles. We vary in our knowledge, skills, and our strength to do these tasks, but we can try, depending on the grace of God and the help of the Holy Spirit.

CLOSING PRAYER: O God: We are thankful that you are the God of Light and Life. We have heard the voice of Jesus calling. You want us to join you, to come out of whatever darkness clouds our lives, to come out and live with you—abundantly, eternally; and you want us to help others to be children of Light. Help us by your Holy Spirit to follow your call. In Jesus' name we pray. Amen.

Questions for Reflection or Discussion

1. Both men and women can be "Mary" and "Martha" type persons. Which are you? Or are you a mixture of the two? Would you like to change? How can you do that?

2. Why is it hard for us to face the reality of death? How can this Scripture help us overcome that fear? What specifically can you do for yourself to conquer or ease the fear? What can you do for others?

3. Can you identify one or more "tombs" or areas of darkness in your life from which you would like to escape? What can you do to move out of that darkness toward the light of life with other people, and with Jesus?

4. Think of someone near you who needs help in moving out of some dark spot into the light of fuller life. What can you do to "roll back the stone" and "untie the bonds" of that person?

Part III
THE TRINITY

GOD IN THREE PERSONS

49

One God:
Father, Son, and Holy Spirit

Deuteronomy 6:4; John 1:14; Romans 5:8; Genesis 1:1-31;
Hosea 11:1-8; Psalm 23; Luke 15:11-24; Jonah 4:2c; Isaiah 44:22

OPENING PRAYER: God of our fathers and of our mothers: We are thankful that we are your children, that you are our parent. We sense your power, we glimpse your glory, we feel your love; and we want to be part of your kingdom. You are too infinite for us to comprehend; too glorious for us to understand. We can never know you and your ways completely. However, what we do know gives our lives support, meaning, and direction. Be close to us as we study your Word in Scripture. Help us to know you better as God the Father, God the Son, and God the Holy Spirit. We pray to you now in the words our Lord Jesus taught us, saying together The Lord's Prayer . . . .

LESSON: We conclude our study of the Bible's Good News with four lessons on the One we sing to as "God in three persons, blessed Trinity." The Church teaches that God is, somehow, *one* Divine Being, and also *three* Persons. This is one of the mysteries of a God who is older, bigger, grander, more glorious and more holy than we can comprehend. Yet we must try, for it is an important aspect of the nature of God's relationship to us.

We believe in *one* God, not many gods, as did the Greeks and Romans. Our belief is supported by a key verse in Deuteronomy, one that is very important to both Jews and Christians: "Hear, O Israel; the LORD is our God; the LORD is one" (Deuteronomy 6:4). The Jews were monotheists, believers in one god. Their God, who is our God, is the Creator of heaven and earth, and of us. This verse says that the Divine Being with this holy personal name is our God, our *only* God; and he is one Being.

We believe that God is one Being, but we also say that God is three Persons. What does that mean? It means that we cannot fully understand God and his ways. His power, holiness, glory, and love are immense—too big for us to grasp fully. We experience only parts of his great wholeness. Yet, as we have learned, he reveals himself to us. He is revealed in Creation, in history, in the Bible, and of course in Jesus. He has revealed, among other things, the three main ways in which he relates to us: as one who creates and governs; as one who forgives and saves; and as one who sustains, empowers, and guides. That is, God the Father, God the Son, and God the Holy Spirit. Here is a brief look at these three ways in which God relates to us.

God the Father is the Creator and giver of life; we are his children. Like the head of a family, God provides for us, takes care of us, and protects us. He instructs us about what we should and should not do. He disciplines us when we do not obey; but his discipline is always just and loving. He may seem distant at times, and that is why he also has revealed himself as God the Son.

God the Son is God the Savior—God in human form, close and friendly; the infinite love of God embodied in Jesus of Nazareth. A part of God "became flesh and lived among us" (John 1:14). God came to earth so we might see, know, and love him, and thus be saved. In Jesus Christ, we see a God of *forgiving* love, one who loves us, even when we do not deserve it. As Paul wrote, "While we still were sinners Christ died for us" (Romans 5:8). He saved us from our sinful selves and thus frees us for new life, as children created in God's own image. After the Resurrection, Jesus returned to the Father and sent an Advocate or helper, the Holy Spirit.

God the *Holy Spirit* inspires, empowers, guides, sustains, and comforts us. We are saved when the Spirit that was in Christ comes to dwell in us. There he inspires and guides. He gives us the power to be the man or woman God created us to be. He travels life's path with us, comforts us, and holds us up when we stumble.

Most of the lessons in this book relate, in one way or another, to God the Father. The rest of this lesson will summarize what we already know about him. When we think of God as Father, we think first of the Creator, the giver of all life, the source of *our* lives. He is our parent; we are his children, created in his own image.

(Read Genesis 1:1-31.) God loves and cares for everything he made. He wants to be in close relationship with all his creatures, especially with us, his children. The prophet Hosea speaks of God as loving and forgiving his people Israel, as a father to a wayward, stumbling son.

(Read Hosea 11:1-4.) The fact that the son "turned away" did not destroy God's love. He wants our relationship to continue. He told us, through the prophet: "How can I give you up, Israel? How can I abandon you? . . . My heart will not let me do it! My love for you is too strong" (11:8 GNB). Like any good father, God nurtures those he loves. We saw this in depth when we studied the 23rd Psalm.

God's fatherhood has another aspect. He instructs us, telling us how to behave. When we do not follow his teaching, he disciplines us. However, his judgment and his love are joined. He is not just a judge who condemns us. Nor does he indulge us to do anything and everything we may want to do. His discipline has a healing quality. He strives to help us become like children created in his image. It sometimes *seems* that the God of the Old Testament is a stern, punishing judge, different from the loving, forgiving God of the New Testament. Actually, careful reading of the whole Bible reveals a Heavenly Father whose discipline *and* forgiveness both flow from the same loving heart.

We now look at New and Old Testament passages which show *one* picture of what God is like. You remember Jesus' parable of a father and his prodigal son. Jesus was saying, "God is like this father, only more so." **(Read Luke 15:20.)** Dad was so happy to have his child back, he celebrated with a big party.

Jonah tells us about the Old Testament God he knew. He did it by quoting a still older voice from the book of Exodus: "You are a loving and merciful God, always patient, always kind, and always ready to change your mind and not punish" (Jonah 4:2 GNB). Did you hear that? *Always* ready to *not* punish—when we "go home."

Finally, listen to the gracious word God spoke to a people he had disciplined by exile in Babylon: "Return to me, for I have redeemed you" (Isaiah 44:22). Like the father of that prodigal son, God says to every one of us who has strayed from his Way, "Come on home, I have already forgiven you!" That is indeed Good News. Praise the LORD!

CLOSING PRAYER: Gracious God, our Father: We are thankful that your loving heart pours out forgiveness for all of us, your children. Your arms are always held out to us, wanting us to come home, to be with you now and in Heaven—forever. We accept your invitation with grateful hearts. Amen.

Questions for Reflection or Discussion

1. Think of specific times when you have experienced God as a parent; as Savior; as Holy Spirit. Were the experiences similar or different? In what ways?
2. Do you respond differently to each of the three Divine Persons? If so, in what ways? If not, why not?
3. What aspects of God's nature as a parent are most important to you? Why?
4. Think of two or three times when you have experienced God's discipline. Was each primarily just? Primarily loving? A combination of the two?

5 0
Jesus of Nazareth:
His Humanness

John 4:6-7; 11:35; Hebrews 4:15; Matthew 4:1-11; 21:12;
Luke 4:13b; Mark 14:32-39, 50, 66-72; Mark 15:34, 37; Psalm 22

OPENING PRAYER: Heavenly Father of our Lord Jesus Christ, and *our* father too: We are thankful for all your many gifts to us; for family and friends, many of whom are already with you in Heaven. We are thankful for a place to eat and sleep; and for people who are interested in our welfare. Most of all, O God, we are thankful for your Son Jesus, who was Divinity in a human body; who came to earth to be one of us, to share our problems, to suffer and die as we do. Because he shared our humanness, he understands us and loves us. So we pray to you, using the words he taught us, saying together The Lord's Prayer . . . .

LESSON: We continue trying to understand the mystery of the Trinity. This lesson focuses on the humanness of Jesus, who called himself the Son of Man, who came to earth and shared our human life. The Church has always taught that the One we call Jesus Christ was at the very same time both completely human and fully divine. That is the doctrine of the Incarnation.

From the earliest days of the Church, there have been two heresies related to Jesus. First, some have believed that Jesus was just a great man: a prophet whose teachings tell us how we should live; a man whose courage shows us how to die for what is right. Just a human being like you and me. This heresy denies Jesus' divinity, and thus takes away belief in a God of love who died for us. Believing only this, we have Jesus as a leader and friend (which we need), but not as a Savior (which we need even more).

The opposite heresy holds that Jesus was totally divine; he only *seemed* to be human. He only seemed to get hungry, tired, angry; only seemed to bleed, only seemed to die. He was not *really* human. To deny Jesus' humanity is to lose a friend who knows and understands us. To believe that Jesus was not fully human denies us a personal relationship with a friendly, loving God. Jesus Christ was—and is—both divine *and* human, both our Savior and our friend.

Now we look at some Scriptures which show that Jesus was indeed completely human. The New Testament tells us that he was tempted. In Hebrews, we read that Jesus intercedes for us in heaven as a High Priest; however, he is *not* one "who is unable to sympathize with our weaknesses, but we have one who in every respect has been tested as we are, yet without sin" (Hebrews 4:15). That is, Jesus knows and understands every human temptation that you and I have. We discussed how the devil gave him three special temptations in the desert. Each tried to use a common human weakness to deflect Jesus from the divine plan for his life. He had to decide what kind of Messiah he would be; decide how to use his very special powers (Matthew 4:1-11). Jesus was human like you and me, yet he followed God's way without faltering, even to the Cross.

The Bible tells of many human experiences which Jesus shared with us. Hot, tired, and thirsty, he asked the woman at the well for a drink of water (John 4:6-7). "Jesus wept" (John 11:35) when his friend Lazarus died. He could get angry, as at the money changers (Matthew 21:12). He was disappointed when his three closest disciples could not stay awake while he prayed in the Garden (Mark 14:37). He knew rejection: when he was arrested, all the disciples ran away (Mark 14:50). Even brave Peter denied him, three times (Mark 14:66-72)!

However, two events at the very end of his earthly life show us his deep essential humanness. The first was Thursday night of Holy Week. Tomorrow would be the Cross. (**Read Mark 14:33-39.**) Just like us, Jesus did not *want* to suffer; the idea of pain and death made him distressed and anguished. Three times he prayed, "Do I *have* to do this? Please, Father, take it away." And three times he prayed, "Not my will but thine be done." His distress and fear were human.

The other event came the next day on the Cross itself. It was about nine o'clock "when they nailed him to the tree." "At three o'clock Jesus cried out with a loud voice, 'Eloi, Eloi, lema sabachthani?' which means, 'My God, my God, why have you forsaken me?' . . . Then Jesus gave a loud cry and breathed his last" (Mark 15:34, 37). It is very human, when in pain and hopeless despair, to feel that we have been abandoned by God. Have not most of us felt that way? According to Mark, at least for a moment, Jesus felt just like we do. But remember that Psalm 22, which Jesus quoted, ends on a note of confident faith in God. Like Jesus, we can be confident of God's love, even in the midst of pain and despair.

CLOSING PRAYER: O God, our Father: Help us to hear and hold close in our hearts the Good News of your saving love for all human beings. Through the Son, the humanness of Jesus, you know and understand our human nature. You know and "sympathize with *all* our weaknesses." For this, and all your many gifts, we are thankful. In Jesus' name and for his sake, we pray. Amen.

Questions for Reflection or Discussion

1. Is it important to you that Jesus is "the human face of God"? Why or why not? In what ways can that be important?
2. How did Jesus deal with his temptations—both his "common" temptations and his "special" ones? Does knowing that help us deal with ours? How?
3. Is it important to you that Jesus Christ is at the same time both "completely human" and "fully divine"? Why or why not?
4. Read all of Psalm 22. Does it describe your experiences? How does this it make you feel about your relationship with the Triune God?
5. Has there been a time in your life when you felt lost in pain and despair? Did you feel forsaken, or confident of God's loving care—or both? Please explain.

51

The Divinity of
the Christ of God

John 1:1-18

OPENING PRAYER: Gracious God: We are thankful that you reveal yourself to us. You are revealed as a God of power and of love. Your power and wisdom are revealed in the Universe you created. Your love and justice are revealed to us through human relationships at their best: parents and children, wives and husbands, all relationships that are governed by your will and way. But Father, your most perfect and complete revelation is Jesus of Nazareth, your specially Anointed One, whom we call the Christ. He shows us that you are, indeed, a God of love—and we are thankful. Therefore, we now pray together as he taught us, saying The Lord's Prayer . . . .

LESSON: The previous lesson emphasized the humanity of Jesus. This lesson emphasizes Jesus' Divinity. The Gospel of John was the last Gospel written. It uses ideas and words familiar to the Greeks of his day. One word important to their philosophers was "Word." To them, the meaning of "word" combined three ideas. A *divine principle* to be realized, to be expressed in nature and in human life. *Revelation*—God reveals himself through his Word. The Word itself is *power.* John's Gospel tells us that Jesus was the Word of God: the divine principle by which the world was created, the revelation of God, and the power of God—God's Incarnation in human form.

(**Read John 1:1-14***a.*) Here are key verses from some modern translations, which try to shed new light on this Gospel's message about Jesus Christ, the Word of God made flesh:

Before the world was created, the Word already existed; he was with God, and he was the same as God. From the very beginining the Word was with God. Through him God made all things; not one thing in all creation was made without him. The Word was the source of life, and this life brought light to mankind. The light shines in the darkness, and the darkness has never put it out. (John 1:1-5 GNB)

This was the real light—the light that comes into the world and shines on all mankind. The Word was in the world, and though God made the world through him, yet the world did not recognize him. He came to his own country, but his own people did not receive him. Some, however, did receive him and believed in him; so he gave them the right to become God's children. (John 1:9-12 GNB)

The Word became flesh and lived among us . . . full of grace and truth. (John 1:14)

Out of the fullness of his grace he has blessed us all, giving us one blessing after another. God gave the Law through Moses, but grace and truth came through Jesus Christ. No one has ever seen God. The only Son, who is the same as God and is at the Father's side, he has made him known. (John 1:16-18 GNB)

Jesus, whom we call Christ and Lord, has made God known to us. Of course, we see God in the world of Nature he created. We hear his voice through the Prophets. We see him in human relationships: in the new life of a baby, in the love of parents and of husbands and wives. We see God's love in *anyone* who cares enough for another person to sacrifice, suffer, perhaps die for the other. God makes himself known in *many* ways. However, Jesus is the most complete revelation of the nature and power of God. Christ revealed God through his teaching, healing, and saving death. We are called by Jesus, the Man and the Christ, to a life of love—for others. It is not easy! But it is *the abundant life, eternal life.*

CLOSING PRAYER: O God, who reigns above, who loves and cares for us: You are never far away; but through all grief distressing, an ever present help and stay, our peace and joy and bless-ing. As with a mother's tender hand, you gently lead your chosen band. To you all praise and glory! Amen. (Adapted from the hymn "Sing Praise to God Who Reigns Above.")

Questions for Reflection or Discussion

1. Is it important to you that Jesus Christ was fully divine, as well as completely human? In what way or ways? Why?
2. "The words of the Bible bear witness to the Word." What does this statement mean? Do you agree? Why or why not?
3. What things did Jesus say or do, or what things happened to him, to convince you that he was Divine?
4. Of the two heresies about Jesus ("He is a great, wonderful human being; but not divine"; "He is a divine being only; he just *seemed* to be human"), which is more likely to be believed by people in the U.S. today? Why? What strengths and what dangers come to people who believe it?

52
The Holy Spirit of God

Genesis 1:1-2; Judges 11:29; Joel 2:28; Micah 3:8;
Mark 1:9-12; Luke 4:14; John 14:26; 16:7-13; Acts 2:3-4;
Romans 12:11; 1 Corinthians 3:16; Galatians 5:22-23a

OPENING PRAYER: Almighty God, Creator of all that exists, whose glory fills the skies: We are thankful that you are a God of love, as well as power. You are the Father who knows and loves us. You sent your Son, Jesus, to live with us and to die for our salvation. You also send your Holy Spirit to be your continuing presence in our lives. We are thankful for all you are, all you have done, all you mean to us gathered here in your name. Together, we pray now with the words Jesus taught us, saying The Lord's Prayer . . . .

LESSON: Our final lesson is on God the Holy Spirit. Most people know and understand more about the Father and Son than about the Holy Spirit (which we used to call the Holy Ghost). A spirit is the inner essence, the basic nature of a person, his or her inner reality. We think of a spirit as being mobile, active; able to move freely and be at work in different places. In the case of God's Spirit, it is able to do its work in *all* places at *all* times. Both Old and New Testaments are full of references to God's Holy Spirit. Here are some of the things they tell us.

First, the Spirit is the creating power of God, active since the very beginning of Creation. "In the beginning when God created the heavens and the earth, the earth was a formless void and darkness covered the face of the deep, while a wind from God swept over the face of the waters" (Genesis 1:1-2).

Second, the same Spirit "comes to" human beings and "dwells in" them. "The spirit of the LORD came upon Jephthah" (Judges 11:29). Jephthah was a military commander who is not very familiar to us. This verse is included to show that God's Holy Spirit comes to *anyone*—in fact, to *everyone*.

Third, to us Christians, it is important that Jesus of Nazareth received the Spirit in a very special way. **(Read Mark 1:9-12.)** "Then Jesus, filled with the power of the Spirit, returned to Galilee" (Luke 4:14). Jesus embodied the Holy Spirit of God more completely than anyone before or since. This Spirit not only confirmed his divine nature, but also became established in him to guide and empower his ministry.

Fourth, the same Spirit that was in Christ is his gift to us and to everyone. As his death drew near, Jesus tried to explain to his disciples what was about to happen and why he would leave them. **(Read John 16:7-13.)** This gift of the Spirit has done two things for us: On Pentecost, it created the Church to continue Jesus' ministry; and it has claimed us for membership in that Church. **(Read Acts 2:3-4.)** They were *all* filled! More than eight hundred years earlier, a prophet had proclaimed. **(Read Joel 2:28.)** The Spirit is a gift of the Father and of the Son to everyone: women and men, old and young.

Finally, what is the nature of the Spirit in relation to us? We read in John's Gospel that the Spirit is our *helper, teacher, guide:* "The Advocate, the Holy Spirit, whom the Father will send in my name, will teach you everything" (John 14:26); "When the Spirit of truth comes, he will guide you into all the truth" (John 16:13). He *empowers* us, gives the ability and strength to live and walk in God's Way. A prophet proclaimed: "The LORD fills me with his spirit and power" (Micah 3:8 GNB). The Spirit *lives in us,* so our lives can bear the *fruits of the Spirit.*

Paul wrote: "Do you not know that you are God's temple and that God's Spirit dwells in you?" (1 Corinthians 3:16); "The fruit of the Spirit is love, joy, peace, patience, kindness, generosity, faithfulness, gentleness, and self-control" (Galatians 5:22-23*a*). When the Holy Spirit lives in us, we are enabled to live up to the image that God created in each of us.

God is with us, in the Person of the Holy Spirit, to inspire, teach, guide, empower, sustain, and comfort. He is with us in joy and sorrow, in pleasure and pain; he is with us in life and in death. *Always.* God is with us. We are not alone. "Thanks be to God!"

SHELTERED BY GOD'S LOVE

CLOSING PRAYER: O God, you are more powerful, wise, and loving that we can fully comprehend. We know and love you, not because we understand you completely, but because *you* know and understand us, because you first loved us. We are thankful that you are always present with us as the Holy Spirit. We are not alone; thank you, LORD. Amen.

Questions for Reflection or Discussion

1. Which do you think is the best name for the Third Person of the Trinity—"Holy Ghost" or "Holy Spirit"? Why?
2. Has the Holy Spirit ever "come to" or "touched" you? If so, what happened? How did you feel? What did you do?
3. What "gifts of the Spirit" have you received? How have you used them?
4. For you personally, is the Spirit more of a guide/teacher, a comforter, or both? Or something else? Please explain.
5. Hymns about the Holy Spirit are probably not as well known as those about God the Father and God the Son. Can you think of any hymns about the Holy Spirit that are meaningful to you, that tell how the Spirit functions in your life?
6. What is the most important thing you have learned from these 52 Bible lessons? Why?